Wilmington, Our Town

A Collection of Memories and Personal Stories by Wilmington Residents

Copyright 2021

ISBN: 9798728487845

(Printed in large 14 point font)

DEDICATION

This book is dedicated to all the wonderful residents of our town, Wilmington, Massachusetts, and to the hundreds of contributors,

With special recognition to:

Emily 'Terri' Peabody

and

Carol Tildsley

"It's my hometown, but it's also a great town. There're lots of stories here when you peel back the layers."
 —Joel Vetsch

A Look Back

This collection of personal stories and past memories are shared by people lucky enough to have grown up in a small, intimate town.

They tell of the early days when life as a child was simple and safe. They talk about the foods they ate and the places they went, of the things they did and the games they played and the schools they loved.

They write about the tiny universe they were raised in, with its lake and creeks and bogs and swamps and woods and trails and fields and farms they explored. They roamed the land as "free range kids" with unbound freedom.

They talk about the people who impacted and influenced their lives: their teachers and coaches, their parents and neighbors. They relive the years with their young friends and close neighbors as if they were family, because they were.

They remember their struggles and hardships, and their good and fun times too. They remember their first loves and old enemies.

But in the end, they look back at those 'good old days' and smile with gratitude that they grew up in *Wilmington, Our Town.*

Foreword
by
Bob Johnson
(WHS Class of 1968)

Wilmington, Our Town

A long time ago there was a secret place where good things happened.

Young families fled there from the inner cities, the crowded streets, and the depressing tenement rentals in search of the American dream. Cab drivers and factory workers and office employees and construction laborers and school teachers and thousands of other hard working, determined people wanted a better life for themselves, their children, and their future grandchildren.

These brave souls traded in their old dank apartment buildings and noisy neighborhoods and perilous streets for an uncertain promise. They bought rundown shanties and tiny cottages along tree-lined back roads and narrow avenues. They fixed up and painted and wallpapered the old summer houses, proudly turning them into cute and quaint personal castles. They marveled at their small pieces of land and their comfortable new homes and their front porches in this fresh world filled with possibilities.

And they felt good about it.

A new and welcomed universe had been discovered in this secret place. The forests were thick and vibrant and full of life. The country air was crisp, blue and clean. The creeks and brooks and the lake were a thousand miles from their past lives. There were no locks on the front doors and night windows stayed open and people watched out for one another.

And more families came.

The children played outdoors from breakfast 'til dusk. They wore hand-me-down clothes and patched dungarees and ate simple suppers and were glad for what they had.

In the springtime they found polliwogs wiggling in the nearby ponds and swamps. They floated on wobbly rafts and got stuck in knee deep mud. They built makeshift forts in the woods and swung on long Tarzan ropes.

In the summer heat they spent most of their time at the popular lake beaches and cashed in soda bottles to score a double scoop ice cream cone. They fished the shallow banks of the lake for perch and bass and sunfish, and catfish in the ponds. They found wild blueberries and hidden strawberries and crabapple trees to munch on as they explored the abundant land.

They saved baseball cards packed with a slab of sweet chewing gum. They played Cowboys and Indians and three-man baseball and Red Rover and Hide-and-Go-Seek. They collected insects and frogs and snakes and lightning bugs in their adventurous days.

As the weather cooled the children walked to school a good distance away, not a care in the world. They played in huge piles of dried leaves from the autumn color, and collected fallen acorns from the grand oaks. They bought and shared ten-cent comic books and handfuls of penny candy with their friends.

In the winter these carefree youngsters built snow fortresses to protect their neighborhood, never noticing the bitter cold. They skated on thin or caked ice wherever it was found. They caught snowflakes with their tongues and snapped dripping icicles from roof edges and slid down snow-packed hills on cardboard sleds.

And the days were good.

At school during the morning attendance, the young students stood and put their right hands over their hearts while reciting the Pledge of Allegiance as their eyes focused on the brilliant American flag in the classroom. They sat for a moment of silence to reflect or offer their personal gratitude without questioning differing beliefs.

And they learned about honor and respect. And they were becoming good people.

When the years slipped by they understood if they wanted anything beyond what their meager weekly allowance could buy, they had to work. There were lawns to mow and driveways to shovel and fences to paint and cars to wash. There were grocery bags to be packed and ice cream cones to be scooped and plates of food to be served.

Money was freedom. It allowed the boys to have beefed-up muscle cars and rusty old clunkers. It made possible new dresses and shoes and stylish fashions. It got the kids to Hampton and Salisbury Beaches and to the drive-in movies and to the dances and to the local hangouts. And their hard-earned paychecks taught them the importance of a strong New England work ethic.

And they began to appreciate life.

In their high school years these young adults formed solid and often long-lasting friendships based on commitment and loyalty. They played football and basketball and baseball and hockey and soccer and track and grasped the concept that sometimes in life they would win and sometimes they would lose.

Then, too quickly their futures demanded decisions guided by principles learned. They went off to college, the ones who could. The smart ones, the daring ones, the lucky ones. Others had different callings and joined the military during a tumultuous and dangerous time. Many gave their lives for what they believed in, and for all it was a hard lesson learned.

Because they all wanted something better.

As they went off to find their purpose in this world, each and every one of these amazing people—children of even more remarkable pioneers—were well prepared. They may have been scared or hesitant or unsure of their future paths, but they were strong and determined and self-thinkers and risk takers.

And they knew they would do well in this world.

They had been taught right and wrong, and inspired to be good by their steadfast parents. They had been watched over by their many uncles and aunts and neighbors to keep them straight. They had been trained and guided by their teachers and pushed by their coaches to instill the very principles of success. They had been blessed by priests and pastors to follow the sacred rules. They had been rightfully held to task by their strict but fair bosses and local shop owners and area police officers. All of whom, through a distinctively innate concern for these community youths, played important parts in the development and growth of these truly remarkable kids.

And these children of this once secret place, this small country town of Wilmington, grew up to be productive, caring, involved individuals.

They grew up to be good people.

I am honored to be among them.

Contents
Stories written, shared, or contributed by:

Brian Norton—"I Saw Bigfoot!"

Frank Stone—A Winning Team

Deborah Shine Harrington—Wilmington Youth Crusaders Drum & Bugle

Michael Barcellos—A Good Man

Terri O'Conners Allum—My Adventurous Brother

Jane Woods—Missing the Good Old Days

Fred Shine—Wilmington's Fallen Heroes

Valerie Clark—Ma's Seven Rules

Shared by Members—Foods We Ate

Brent Clark—Poole's Bakery

Sandra Wilson—Our Early Days

Tony Kissel—Life on Butters Row

Debbie Harrington—A Thanksgiving Memory

Fred Shine—Fallen Heroes: Part I
The Richard Welch Memorial

Frank Stone—Olympic Medal Winner

Wilmington Residents—Places We Went

Larz Neilson—Weinberg's

Tony Meads—My Neighborhood

Brent Clark—A Long Hike to Silver Lake

Joe Casey—Hanging Out & Muscle Cars

Cathy Seely—My Wilmington Family

Dianna DiGregorio—A Look at Wilmington History

Marjorie Campbell—Saving Wilmington Arts

Group Conversation—Free Range Kids

Fred Shine—Fallen Heroes: Part II In Honor of John J. Fullerton

Carol Day Boisvert—The Day Family and Wilmington

Survivors' Memories—The Blizzard of '78

Fred Shine—Blizzard Problems

Christine E. Goodwin—Butters Farm

Active Youths—Games We Played

Linda Arsenault—Mr. Sparks, A Fire Escape, & Me

The Group—My Mother Told Me…

Peggy Speranza—Life at the Lake

Tony Kissel—Wilmington High School

Joyce (Eaton) Dalton—The Early Years

Brent Clark—Apple Blossoms

Group's Memories—Wilmington's Old Library

Kathy Lawrence Huesgen—Classroom Troubles

Terri Enos Johnston—A Love Song

Fred 'Skip' Shine—Skip and the Gang

Shared Memories—Things We Did

Leisa Park—The Park Family

Tom Mirisola—No Parking

Group Conversation—Our Wilmington Teachers

Larry Gallagher—Getting Around (Trolleys, Trucks, Tricycles, Hikes & Bikes)

Bob Johnson—The Right Thing

Joyce (Eaton) Dalton—Everyday Fun

Carolyn Giannotti—Memories & Changes

Margie Campbell—Nightly Ghosts

Tom Mirisola—The Real Spirit of Our Small Town

Martha Dimond—Little Town in the Country

Beverly O'Connell—Good Times in the Country

Michael Barcellos—Hermit in the Woods

Charlen Landry—Days in Early Wilmington

Fred Shine—Fallen Heroes: Part III
A Tribute to Robert Parent

Past Students—Schools We Knew

Christine Jillett—Polliwogs and Oil Barrels

Charles Fleming—Teachers Teaching

Christine Jillett—Near and Dear to my Heart

Janis Jaquith—THE LANDERS FIRE

Donna White Simard—Back to School

Elaine DePasquale—A Look at Early Wilmington

Chuck Burns—Old Friends

Alison (Francis) Phaneuf—"Come up and see me some time."

Becky Lightizer—The Best Neighborhood

Hank Devlin—"Thank You Wilmington"

Pam Blais—The Great Escape

Fran McLean Donovan—Honorary Mayor of Wilmington

Kathleen O'Brien Weber—Bullied

Karen Lautz Farrell—"When Neighbors Were Like Family"

Donald Hudson—Shenanigans

Fred Shine—Fallen Heroes: Part IV A Salute to John Rich

Denise (Lynch) Robarge—The Egg Route

Ryan Tildsley—Mrs. T

Those Who Cared—Making a Difference

Bob Johnson—Final Thoughts

Book Contributors (275)
(* full story, comments by others)

A Terri O'Conners Allum* ▪ Linda Arsenault* ▪ Erin Antinarell ▪ Linda Aspeslagh ▪ Sydna Anderson ▪ Andrea Aprile ▪ Jeanne Cariglio Abraham

B Michael Barcellos* ▪ Carol Day Boisvert*▪ Chuck Burns* ▪ Pam Blais* ▪ Dennis Blair ▪ Paul Bielecki ▪ Michele Bee* ▪ Tom Beaton ▪ Laura Blair ▪ Kathy Boylen ▪ Janet M. Beyer ▪ Nancy Hall Bull ▪ Doreen Case Buckmore ▪ John Bernard ▪ Mark Bartnick ▪ Elizabeth Briana ▪ Ann Berghaus ▪ Kathleen Bell ▪ Kevin Burke ▪ Paul Burke ▪ Marc Bliss ▪ Barbara Bianchi ▪ Stevie Bee ▪ Mark Bouvier ▪ Terrijoan Marden Bello ▪ Ann Barry ▪ Steve Brown ▪ Dottie Bryn ▪ Claire O'Beirne Brady ▪ Maureen Deveau Bedrosian ▪ Kim Cullivan Baron

C Valerie Clark* ▪ Brent Clark* ▪ Joe Casey* ▪ Margie Campbell* ▪ Rose Chase ▪ Sandra Enos Conwell ▪ Leanne Cummings ▪ Carol Case ▪ Mary Carter ▪ Elizabeth Gilligan Cavanaugh ▪ Susan Carlson ▪ Kathy Christensen ▪ Diane Clifton ▪ Gary Carter ▪ Ed Carrasco ▪ Bernadette

Collins ▪ Gail Ciardi ▪ Shannon Turner Cassidy ▪ Lori A. Ingersoll Carlo
Lisa Kennedy Cox ▪ Douglas Clark ▪ Steve Cavanaugh ▪ Jane Swisher Cannizaro ▪ Lisa Bernard Coolbaugh

D Dianna DiGregorio* ▪ Martha Dimond* ▪ Elaine DePasquale* ▪ Hank Devlin* ▪ Fran McLean Donovan* ▪ Joyce (Eaton) Dalton* ▪ Lorraine Dineen ▪ Diane Dizacomo* ▪ Michael DiGregorio ▪ Patty Jaquith Dineen ▪ John Doucette ▪ Debbie Donovan ▪ Doug Dayton ▪ Lisa DiCecca ▪ Chris DiCecca ▪ John Dineen ▪ Becky Dixon ▪ Kathleen DelRossi ▪ Robin Anderson Downs ▪ Gail Donovan ▪ Bryan Davey ▪ Eileen D'Eon Fenick ▪ Paul Davey ▪ Tom DeLetter

E Bonnie Eagle ▪ Robert Eagan

F Charles Fleming* ▪ Karen Lautz Farrell* ▪ Leslie Freeman* ▪ Sandra Berrigan Fallica ▪ Jacqueleen Fonseca ▪ Betty Woodland Foumier ▪ Carol Freeman Fraser ▪ Lois Freeland ▪ Dee Silverman Fransman ▪ Nancy Fudge ▪ Stephen Gustus ▪ Anne Forrestall ▪ Donna Murray Follett ▪ Kathy Burke Fulmer

G Larry Gallagher* ▪ Christine E. Goodwin* ▪ Mary Lou Govoni ▪ Terry Gustus ▪ Mary Winnett

Giroux* ▪ Carol Bender Gaffney ▪ Kathleen Gilligan ▪ Barry Garden ▪ Lois Hinxman Grant* ▪ William Gustus ▪ Karen Newcomb Giaquinta

H Deborah Shine Harrington* ▪ Kathy Lawrence Huesgen* ▪ Donald Hudson* ▪ Michelle Giroux Higgs ▪ Donald C. Hubbard ▪ Janet Witham Hawes ▪ Mark Hall ▪ Lindsay Currier Hurley ▪ Jim Hachey ▪ Linda Hall

I Jeff Irwin ▪ Diana Murray Isqur

J Bob Johnson* ▪ Christine Jillett* ▪ Janis Jaquith* ▪ Trish Jennings ▪ Lee A. Jewels ▪ Thomas Jillett

K Tony Kissel* ▪ Sandy Longo Keeley ▪ Sharon Kelley ▪ Dave Knight* ▪ Linda Kovitch ▪ Janice Kearney ▪ George Keith ▪ Carolyn M. Kenney ▪ Tracy Russo Knickle ▪ Kimberley Keller ▪ Cindy Leathe Kuehl ▪ Paul Keough ▪ Ellen Balser Kimble

L Becky Lightizer* ▪ Sammy Lunt* ▪ Andrew Leverone ▪ Laurie Carrasco Lowman* ▪ Nancy London ▪ Ellen EJ Lefavour ▪ Michelle Lee ▪ Charlen Landry* ▪ Harry Landers* ▪ Jack Lee ▪ Joann Lucas ▪ Dottie Pike Lyons ▪ Jane Loveys ▪ Ken Liston ▪ Tori Larkin ▪ AnnMarie Barry Legg

▪ Susan Lomastro ▪ Bobby Lanzillo

M   Tony Meads* ▪ Tom Mirisola* ▪ Janet Wesinger Moro ▪ Robin Marsh* ▪ Brian McCue ▪ Bob Murphy ▪ Dorene Messieri ▪ Cheryl Marr ▪ Kathy Menne ▪ Clyde McKaba ▪ Sue Landers McNamara ▪ AnnMarie Mahoney ▪ Daniel Moegelin ▪ Maureen Monroe ▪ Janet McGinley ▪ Janice McLean Moegelin ▪ Bob Moore ▪ Ann McGaffigan ▪ Janice Murray ▪ Peter Mullarky ▪ Dolly Muir-Pierce ▪ Ted McKie ▪ Marilyn Thackeray McGrath ▪ Barbara Mahoney ▪ Mimi McCabe McHugh ▪ Michael McCoy ▪ Mary Ann Magee McKeen

N   Brian Norton* ▪ Larz Neilson* ▪ Joyce Noonan ▪ Don Noonan ▪ Rick Norton

O   Beverly O'Connell* ▪ Karen Oteri ▪ Peter Orlando ▪ Doris O'Connell ▪ Mary Olshaw-Hynes ▪ Bonnie Olson

P   Leisa Park* ▪ Alison (Francis) Phaneuf* ▪ Renee Pineau ▪ Susan Patterson ▪ Merrill Poloian ▪ Mary Ellen Powers ▪ Shirley Pumfrey ▪ Karin Passmore ▪ Ed Palino ▪ Judith Condrey Palm ▪ Beth Ritchie Pidgeon ▪ Patty Poloian Park ▪ Deidre Kelley Perrin ▪ Deb Phillips ▪ Denise LaRivee Pivarnik ▪ Ed Patenaude Sr. ▪ Lu-Ann

Pozzi ▪ Joan Arsenault Phillips ▪ Jacqui Pappalardo

Q Charmagne Quenan

R Denise (Lynch) Robarge* ▪ Martha Rose ▪ Barbara Reinhart-Fitzgerald ▪ Doreen Scolastico Riley ▪ Lillian Halpin Robinson ▪ Vincent Ruggiero ▪ Lori Rankin ▪ Terry Riel

S Frank Stone* ▪ Fred Shine* ▪ Cathy Fantasia Seely* ▪ Peggy Speranza* ▪ Donna White Simard* ▪ Charlotte Steward ▪ Brandee Walden Stigman ▪ Lisa St. Hilaire ▪ Deborah Hall Shanteler ▪ Tanya Coy Shiner ▪ Lisa Stira ▪ Alice (Chisholm) Shaffer ▪ Colin Scovil ▪ Cindi Richards Stratton ▪ Barbara A. Smith ▪ Alice B. Stone ▪ Patricia Sullivan ▪ Rosemary Smith

T Kathy Whitney Timmons ▪ Patricia Toner ▪ Joe Thiel ▪ Alice Anderson Tobiassen ▪ Lauren Tuner-Cigna ▪ Janice Ritchie Taylor ▪ Bill Trites ▪ Ryan Tildsley

V Jack Virtus

W Jane Woods* ▪ Sandra Wilson* ▪ Kathleen O'Brien Weber* ▪ Leanne Bishop Woodland ▪ Bryan Webster ▪ Bob Wolley ▪ Betty Webb ▪ Mary Whitcomb ▪ Deborah White ▪ Terry

Walden ▪ Lusann Wishart ▪ Betsy Walters ▪ Tom Walsh ▪ Bob Welch ▪ Kathleen Wagstaff ▪ Robin Woodland ▪ Darlene Dalessio Whitney ▪ Susan Taylor Given Wass ▪ Bryan Webster

Z Linda Landry Zwan

Wilmington, Our Town

"I Saw Bigfoot!"
Story shared by Brian Norton

Legends over the years remain alive and well into the modern era.

The Loch Ness monster still inhabits a deep lake in the Scottish Highlands. The Yeti, or Abominable Snowman, lives in the Himalayan snow-covered mountains. Mermaids swim the oceans, fairies flutter in Japan, and leprechauns appear in rural Ireland.

Well, you get the idea.

Whether myth, folklore, or reality, these stories of strange creatures living among us continue to survive. A group of Wilmington school kids believed what they saw and tell their story.

Back in the winter of 1977, youngsters in the Shawsheen area of town were playing in the surrounding woods after school. They often spent time there, not far from their homes, to explore the forest. They found sticks worthy of sword fighting. They climbed trees with low hanging branches to get a bird's eye view of the region.

They raced along the trails and threw rocks at birds and squirrels, never hitting their marks.

Running along the slippery foot path covered with packed snow, eleven-year old Brian Norton fell to the ground. His friends were behind him. Right before him in the mix of wet leaves and snow and thick mud he saw an imprint stomped into the earth and snow. It was huge. Like a human footprint, only larger. At quick glance it looked to be about a foot and a half long and twice as wide as any man's foot.

The other kids at first laughed at Brian's tumble. Then, seeing the thick impression in the hardened ground, they pulled back.

"What is that?" one of them asked, his eyes big with curiosity.

"It's Bigfoot!" one of the boys yelled. The company of children looked at each other. A sense of natural fear spread among the group.

There was a crackle of snapped branches up ahead. Critters in the woods. Maybe. The sun was receding and long shadows stretched through the forest. No kid in his or her right mind wanted to be in the woods after dark. The blowing winter wind swayed loose branches and stirred up dried leaves. Tree silhouettes and dark images cast their movements in the distance.

This was enough for the children's imagination to break loose. One of the young boys said he had recently watched a program on television about the elusive monster known as

Bigfoot in the dense, uninhabited forests of Washington State.

The giant footprint had a deep heel mark and clear toe impressions. Nearer the Shawsheen River, young Tina Ozman and Barbara Donovan saw something in the water. Later they said it appeared to be a ten foot tall ape-like creature.

The children turned and ran as fast as they could toward their homes. Lisa Perry was the first to run for her life. Their pumping hearts and sense of survival told them to get out of there now.

From inside their friend Kevin Donovan's house, several sets of eyes were convinced they could see the mysterious creature through the reflective windows. Barry Fredericks was certain he had seen the big hairy monster.

Figuring no one outside the actual witnesses would not believe what they had seen, Brian went to the town's newspaper, the Town Crier. In a very excited and animated voice he relayed what he and his friends had seen in the woods. No doubt the reporter listened with cynicism, but thought it good sport to write the colorful tale.

When sharing this story Brian said, "My friend Kevin Donovan hyped me up and I started believing it. I was convinced that it was true." Soon the neighborhood was buzzing and the other kids thought they had seen the creature as well.

But in the end there really wasn't any Bigfoot in Wilmington near the Shawsheen River. The practical joker, sweet little fellow student Mary Ann Frederick, was suspected in creating the oversized creature foot impression and simply waited for her friends to freak out.

Good one, Mary Ann.

A Winning Team

Story shared by Coach Frank Stone

Softball is a favorite sport in America played by athletes of all ages, from young children to school aged students, up to active adult leagues and even senior clubs. It's a perfect weekend outing for the casual player, a backyard ball game for the neighborhood kids, or a spirited game of talent and strategy in its most competitive form.

In 1980 a truly exceptional group of young softball players from the small town of Wilmington, Massachusetts, set their sites on achieving something that had never been done. Comprised of a bunch of area eleven and twelve year old girls whose last names were familiar in the township tucked away from the larger regional cities, their top-notched team was destined for greatness.

These young athletes had played their hearts out on the fields. All through the season they had won many difficult matches and had lost their share of contests. They had played against each other throughout the summer, both rivals and friends. They had cheered for their teammates and cried at the disappointments. They had starred as individual ball players and toiled as team units. But, each and every one of these young ladies persevered. Their goal was to play the best they could and to win.

During the regular softball season thousands of ball players had represented their local teams and different leagues. But in all sports particular stars shine. The best of the best prove their worthiness to enter the more challenging competitions.

And so, the town of Wilmington had selected the top young contenders from the local teams to compete in the Massachusetts State Tournament. The youthful athletes were thrilled to be chosen to play in such a prestigious event. Their friends and families and teammates were nearly as excited at the prospect of playing against other state lineups.

The all-star roster included some of the hottest players ever fielded on a diamond. It included: outstanding pitchers, Kim Mytch and Val Sullivan, backed up by great hitters and defenders from Nancy Fillio, Gail Lombard, Yvonne Lesko, Renee Gilson, Kathy Robinson, Tami McDonald, Becky Batten, Sandy Berrigan, Andrienne

Sartori, Leigh Hasting, Lori Ross, and Kelly Deluca.

The small town elite team was rightfully managed by nominated seasoned coaches, Bud Callahan and Frank Stone. After ten years of coaching softball teams, these men persisted in having their players put forth their best efforts. They often reminded the girls they were there to have fun as well.

The Wilmington team had played six games in the tournament, eliminating teams in their way, including a strong Worcester club. They had defeated very good teams and ended up winning the coveted state title. Then they went on to compete in the New England play-offs.

Finally, going up against the solid Connecticut squad, the local all-stars were beaten. In the end, Connecticut nearly won the countrywide title, but had succumbed to California in the very last game.

The local girls' dreams of winning the championship had been dashed. The ride back home was a long one with tears in their eyes and frustration on their faces. But their leaders, their mentors, their coaches, Bud and Frank filled with pride, reminded their players that life wasn't always about winning. It was mostly about simply showing up and doing the absolute best they possibly could.

And they had.

> **Remember when...**
> ...you picked up the kitchen wall phone and heard people talking on the other end

Wilmington Youth Crusaders Drum & Bugle Corps
Story contributed by
Deborah Shine Harrington

I grew up in Wilmington on Grove Ave. across from Baby Beach at Silver Lake. We lived one house away from Tats, the popular mom and pop store. In my earlier years I went to the Mildred H. Rogers School located next to Town Beach.

That alone was a great start to my childhood, however, back then in this small town I had nothing to do.

Enter Roy and Ruth Wallace of North Wilmington and the Wilmington Youth Crusaders Drum and Bugle Corps. The Wallaces were the driving force to the Corps being in Wilmington. You didn't need to know how to march or play the bugle or pound a drum or carry a flag, a rifle, or a saber. You just had to want to belong. Everything else the instructors taught you.

The first time I ever saw the Corps was at the 4th of July parade in Wakefield. That school year two of my friends were joining and wanted me to join as well. So, we went to the American Legion building on Middlesex Ave. and a new world opened.

In the early years we competed all over New England, but rarely placed in the top three. Practices were held weekly. On holidays we marched in parades. We held military balls and played at softball games. On Saturday nights we went roller skating and had dances.

Ohhhh, but on summer nights we were on the competition field under the lights in front of thousands of Drum and Bugle Corps fans. Wearing that uniform, hearing our Corps' name announced, the appreciation of the crowd for a performance well done, it's nothing you can put into words.

In 1969 we won the Mayflower Circuit Championship. We came back to a thrilling Homecoming Parade in honor of our victory. We took second place in the Eastern Massachusetts Circuit. We also took ninth place in the World Open, a two-day competition against corps from all over the states and Canada.

Members weren't just Wilmington kids anymore. They came from towns like Millis, Fitchburg, Needham, Tewksbury, Billerica, North Reading, Dracut and Lowell, to name a few. We traveled on school buses, slept on gym floors, and had friends in corps from other towns and states.

Returning home from the shows sometimes (most times) wasn't until the wee hours of the morning. But we got off the buses, grabbed our instruments and equipment, and played our routine in the vacant lot. If you happened to live near Wilmington Plaza you probably were woken up around two in the morning. If you were, and are reading this now, sorry. (Not really!)

It was the best times for us. People did call the town police because of the noise, but the officers were great and would take the 'long' way around so we could finish before they told us to go home.

We learned a ton from the Drum and Bugle Corps while having fun: teamwork, responsibility, the importance of discipline and friendship. All skills we continue to use throughout our lives. Thanks so much to the Wallaces, our instructors, and all the supportive parents.

The Crusaders created friendships for a lifetime.

"I can remember as a member of the Wilmington Youth Crusaders Drum and Bugle Corps the two women who instructed us. Unfortunately, after all these years I can't remember their names," **Rosemary Smith** recalls. "We used to practice a lot. We had our beautiful uniforms and batons and flags, and of course our instruments.

"Our entire group traveled to other cities and competed against other drum and bugle corps. It was fun to contend against the other teams. Every so often there would be a sleepover for us girls. It was such an enjoyable time."

A Good Man

Written by Michael Barcellos
WHS Class of 1975

My name is Michael Barcellos. I have been a resident of Wilmington since sometime in 1957, when as an infant my family moved here from Cambridge, Massachusetts.

My grandfather, Dr. Manuel de Barcellos, had been a doctor at Central Hospital in Somerville (where I was born) before he moved to Wilmington in 1955 to set up his private practice closer to his daughters. He had been born in the Azores, Portugal, and came to the U.S. in 1902. He went to Boston College, then the University of Kansas City, for his MD degree. He practiced in Somerville before coming to Wilmington.

When my mother was pregnant with me, my grandfather (who was also her doctor) detected something was wrong. At forty years old in 1957 a pregnancy was uncommon and any problems early on needed to be immediately attended to.

Grandfather determined I was "breech" and proceeded to attempt to massage my mother's stomach to help get me into position for delivery. Just before I was born, though, my grandfather was admitted into the hospital where he had been diagnosed with lung cancer.

He must have known this for awhile, and to this day I believe that precipitated his move to Wilmington. My mother began bleeding and was rushed to the hospital. The attending physician consulted my grandfather while he was dying in his hospital bed at New England Baptist Hospital.

When my father spoke to mom's physician, the good doctor said, "I have no knowledge of your wife's situation, but will do as your father (my grandfather) has suggested. I will try to save one of them."

I was born on October 25, 1957. My grandfather died on November 11th, just seventeen days later. My mother lived eighty-eight years.

My dad, Frank D. Barcellos, worked hard as a tool salesman for Snap-on Tools after being a mechanic for many years and serving in the military during WWII.

My story isn't directly related to any of my family, but I thought I'd give you some perspective of how I grew up. First, my sister stands out in Wilmington High School lore as she was 'Miss WHS 1964' and captain of the football cheerleaders. I was an 'ok' athlete and student in Varsity Baseball, graduated from Northeastern University with a BS, and then Lesley University with an MS degree in Business Management.

But my story is about someone who also stood tall in my life besides my grandfather, my parents, my sister and the rest of my family. His name is Larry Noel.

Larry and his wife Dottie had three children: Ray, Bob, and a daughter, whose name unfortunately, I did not know. Tragically the Noel family home had a horrific fire.

Larry was able to save his children, except for his young daughter. His efforts left his arms and other parts of his body terribly burned with scars and sores that haunted him all his life.

But that didn't stop Larry.

He coached his sons in sports and supported them in everything they were involved in. I was a few years behind them in school, so I didn't play Little League with them. But later I played softball in the competitive Wilmington modified fast-pitch league. Even though his boys were no longer in Little League, Larry still coached the kids of Wilmington.

In 1970, my first and only year playing with the Orioles in the town league, (my parents had kept me out of Little League for two years, as it interfered with their trips to Cape Cod). Larry was my coach for the Orioles. He was a big, tall, proud man with a loud thunderous voice and a loud booming laugh.

To a young kid he seemed intimidating until he flashed his big smile and laughed. I knew there was as big a heart inside him even before I learned the genesis of his scars and bandages.

I was pitching in a game against our rivals, the Indians. It was a close game when I came up to bat. I don't recall the inning. Danny Hurley, now a retired Wilmington firefighter, was pitching against us. I swung at a pitch and missed, making the count 3 balls-2 strikes.

I must have looked bad in my swing because Coach Larry from the dugout yelled out to me, "Mikey, get over here!" Shaking a bit, I walked over to my coach.

"What size bat are you using?" he asked in his deep tone. I showed him the largest bat we had, which I was using. He snatched it out of my hand briskly and said, "Give me that." He then handed me a lighter bat and said, "Here, use this."

In his stern manner he looked me in the eye and said, "Now get up there and swing like you mean it!"

I returned to the batter's box. The next pitch came and I swung like I meant it. The ball went flying high over the fence in left field for my first of two home runs that year. It was "magical" to me. When I finished rounding the bases I was greeted by that big smile and pat on the back.

I still have that ball today, fifty years later. It has Larry's signature on it!

That year we had a really solid all-star team, with Kevin Nolan and Charlie Sullivan, among other standouts. We went to the Little League State Finals, finishing a respectable third in the state. Even though I was an alternate who traveled with the team, Mr. Noel made sure **all** the kids received the special Little League pins they awarded the players. He was that kind of guy.

Many years later after college and a family and work and life, I saw Mr. Noel at a Wilmington Fourth of July Celebration. Time had not been kind to him. He was in a wheelchair and had a hard time communicating, but he knew who I was, and I was able to see that big smile once again.

I thought back on that moment in Little League. I thought about how much that time had meant to me. I remembered how it gave me a great boost of confidence in my life that all twelve-year old kids can use as they approach the next stages of their lives, the teen years and beyond.

I don't recall when, but after seeing him at the Wilmington Common I bought a greeting card. A simple 'Thank You' card. In it I wrote about the "magical" home run and let Larry know how much that moment, and he, had meant to my life. I mailed it off and never heard back from his family about it.

When Larry passed away I attended his wake. When I got up to his casket and knelt to pray I looked up to see the card I had sent him so many years ago. It was proudly displayed in the casket.

I couldn't believe it.

When I got up to let others pay their respects, Coach Larry's wife Dottie and his sons, Ray and Bob, were standing there with tears in their eyes......and my eyes as well. After hugs they proceeded to tell me how that card had meant the world to him.

It amazed me how such a small effort on my part had given someone so deserving, a light and a moment of happiness in a life that had been so hard. They asked me if I would give a eulogy the next day and re-live that Little League moment in his memory.

Which I did proudly.

Remember when...
...Arthur Barnaby got a standing ovation during the 1971 graduation ceremony

My Adventurous Brother

Story by
Terri O'Conners Allum

My brother Jim O'Conners graduated from WHS in 1975. He worked as a math substitute teacher in town and Shawsheen Tech for a few years. He later taught at Plymouth Carver High and Turners Falls High.

Always adventurous, Jim was teaching in Shanghai, China when our Mom passed away suddenly in 1993, so he came home for a short visit. Jim went on to teach in Nagoya, Japan, and had to come home once again when Dad passed.

In 1997 my brother went to Bangkok, Thailand, to teach math and coach basketball. Last July he returned home for a month's visit. It was the first time I had seen him in several years. We had a terrific visit.

He left, and that time traveled to Nigeria, Africa to continue teaching math until he decided to retire. We stay in touch only by email and keep each other updated on the Boston sports teams, which we both loved to attend as teenagers.

Missing the Good Old Days

Told by Jane Woods

I remember those days and wish they would come again! Never to be, though.

I now know how my grandmother and grandfather felt watching the changes and longing for yesteryear.

I now know how my mother feels! Losing her sister and feeling the loneliness and longing for a happier and simpler life.

I am now thinking more about my life growing up in Wilmington and how much nicer it was. So uncomplicated and honest and forgiving.

I wish that I could go back and live knowing what I know now.

I long for people to be kind to one another again and not because it's a trend, but because it's in their hearts and it's how they were brought up to be.

Remember when…
…no one locked their front doors at night

Wilmington's Fallen Heroes
The Beginning
by Fred Shine

I remember on Memorial Day the new Wilmington Library was always 'Rededicated' and a wreath was placed in front of the flag pole outside. But I never knew why this was done.

When I first began plans to honor four local boys killed in Vietnam it was brought to my attention that no monuments were needed because the town already had one dedicated to the young boys killed in action. I was told the library was named in their honor.

I asked where the monument was and learned it was actually inside the library. So, one day I went in and looked for it. After walking around and around I asked the girl at the front desk where it was. She pointed toward a wall, hidden pretty much from sight, where a small bronze marker with the names of the four young men, honoring them as 'Men of the Year,' was placed.

If you weren't searching for the plaque you'd never know it existed. To me that was just unacceptable! But over time, whenever I mentioned any type of Vietnam Memorial for these fallen heroes, I was met with hostility (mostly from Korean Vets who had no monument), and two particularly prominent men for their out-spoken disagreement on Vietnam memorials.

One was Ruddy C, and the other was the arrogant Commander of the VFW, Sonny P, who was also known as 'Fudgie'. We locked heads on many occasions and they both found out I could be very stubborn and wouldn't be bullied away.

Growing up at Silver Lake, if you remember, there was a group of pretty tough guys and gals called 'The Rat Traps.' This gang was usually suspected of being behind any mischievous events happening in Wilmington. They wore leather jackets, pointed shoes, iridescent shirts, skin tight pants, and their hair combed back, heavy on the Brylcreem and pointed in the front.

They were known to get into a lot of fights and loved to bully other kids. Especially kids who wore white jeans with the bottom cuffs cut off, penny loafers or sneakers, and Madras shirts. Like me! We were called the 'Clicks.' I was always one of their favorite targets because I was not allowed to fight. IF I did, my Dad would give me a whooping.

Things change, though, when you go in the military. Especially when you end up in a place like Vietnam. You learn very fast to defend yourself and you no longer allow yourself to get pushed. War changes people. Although I never looked for fights, if one found me the outcome was much different than when I was in high school.

That's where I really learned to be stubborn and never backed down from anything I was committed to. And I committed myself to make certain my friends were honored properly, regardless of who I had to fight and no matter what I had to do.

My thought was to put up monuments to my friends, but I needed to find prominent spots worthy of their sacrifice. I wanted respectful memorials, not just some corner street signs with their names on it. I wanted something permanent, something their families and friends would be proud of, something I would be proud enough to say I did it and no one stopped me.

I had heard from an old classmate, Lenny Gustus, about Richard Welch's mother's fight with the town of Wilmington and the state, after Richard died. It seemed the state had plans to expand Route 129, by Bridge Lane, and widen the road with a bridge that would go directly over the Welch's home.

The state wanted to purchase their home, but Millie, Richard's mother, didn't want to sell. It was all she had left after Richard was killed and her husband had died. State Representative Fred F. Cain told her if she didn't sell, the state would just take her home by Eminent Domain. He told her the bridge would be named after someone who would be more deserving than her son who was killed in Vietnam, despite his receiving a Silver Star for bravery in combat.

Millie finally agreed to sell, and the 129 expansion went on. The completed bridge got its new name. It was named, "The Fred F. Cain" Bridge.

Lenny and others tried to get that changed, but were told since Richard was ONLY a private and not a sergeant or lieutenant, it was more fitting to be named after a State Representative and town 'celebrity.'

That's when I got really pissed off and decided I would put up a monument to Richard Welch that would open eyes in town and properly give the Welch family the honor they deserved. However, with the town against me, I had to find an appropriate piece of land to buy, raise money to buy it, and money to build a monument. It had to be someplace special to the family. Someplace that had meaning, and someplace that was NOT hidden from sight!

The search was on, and so plans for the Richard W. Welch monument began!

GOD BLESS AMERICA

Ma's Seven Rules

by Valerie Clark
WHS Class of 1977

One thing imperative to living somewhat peacefully in a house full of ten children is household rules.

Each rule was given more or less as a guideline to teach a value, as well as providing some sort of organization in our large household. We did not have many rules, but each one was very, very important, and breaking one led down the path of "or else." No one in the family had any particular interest in going there with my mother.

Rule #1: Never open someone's mail, listen to their telephone calls, or eavesdrop, and never open a door if it is closed without receiving a response to enter.

This was a pretty simple rule, but essential in teaching each of us the importance of respecting each other's privacy and space.

Rule #2: There would be absolutely no fist fighting within the house. If Ma saw the boys arguing, she would simply tell them to take it outside, and of course, they would.

Rarely did I see any child in our house growing up raise a hand to another in the family. If Ma witnessed an argument she would make sure each party apologized and made up. She promoted being considerate and having empathy for other peoples' feelings. Ma always reminded us to be nice and love each other, because each other was all we had.

Rule #3: Ma expected us to be honest with others and ourselves. She would always cause us to examine our behaviors and actions to learn how to tell the truth. From the beginning, she had her eye on the objective. She was on a mission to raise productive and responsible adults.

It was not a popularity contest. She did not pretend to be our buddy or our friend. She was our mother and our mentor. Ma saw her job as guiding her kids into making wise decisions and steering us through the trials of our teenage years and into the throws of adulthood.

Rule #4: Everyone had chores that were to be done by the time Ma came home for dinner. If the chores were not done she would blow her stack, or worse yet, without a word she would turn around and go back out to the car and drive away.

We would all scurry then to finish up before she returned home. We learned to be responsible for what our tasks were and learned quickly that life was not a free ride. By the age of five the girls could serve a cold supper. By ten or so we could use the top of the stove with supervision, and the same at twelve with the oven. The girls' chores were mostly kitchen and living area duties. The boys tended mainly to the outside chores, including stoking the wood and coal furnace in the cold months.

Rule #5: Ma always demanded impeccable manners. Though, in retrospect I believe she was much more lenient with us kids than her English mother was with her and her own siblings.

She stuck to the basics: Please, Thank You, and Excuse Me. At the dinner table there was no reaching over anyone else's plate or eating until everyone was present. We were taught to chew with our mouths closed and not to speak or interrupt while chewing.

When I was very young I can remember the boys opening doors for her or my sisters, or standing up to offer a chair when an elder entered the room. There is something about good manners that makes people feel good and also makes for extremely good first impressions. Ma felt that manners were imperative to showing respect toward each other and elders.

Rule #6: My mother expected each and every one of us to be accountable and responsible. We were responsible for our own school work and chores, and we were accountable if that did not happen.

When I was around six years old Ma would sometimes hand me some money and send me up over the railroad bridge, down the long set of stairs at the Wilmington train station, and across the parking lot to Poole's Bakery to buy a loaf of fresh bread. I always felt like a big, responsible kid. Little did I know that I was being followed by one of my older siblings.

Rule # 7: Whatever you do, do the best you can and, whatever you do, be the best at being you. Ma always expected us children to work hard at anything we did. Whatever we were to put our hands to do, we were to do it well.

This thought pattern brought about a very important factor. In her infinite wisdom, Ma was teaching us independence, self-respect, and to be proud of who and what we are, and who were would become.

Without a doubt, these have been valuable lessons in mine and my brothers' and sisters' lives as we grew up in the small town of Wilmington.

Excerpt from the book *A Planter's Seed,*
A Tale of Morals, Ethics and Values of My
Mother, Nancy H. Clark, aka: Nosey Nancy

Written and copyrighted by her daughter Valerie Clark

Remember when...
...you opened the new cereal box looking for the prize toy inside
---

Foods We Ate

Shared by Members

Remembering the great foods in our lives triggers visions of good times with good people. The foods we enjoyed as youngsters back in the day may have been simple, but they were real. Wilmington residents, both present and past, share brief comments about the fabulous foods we grew up with.

- Cooking fried bologna sandwiches
- Taking a lunch break at the Rexall Drug store food counter
- Picking blueberries by the train station at the lake

- Making a run with the Uncles up to Jade East for a weekend feast
- Eating the best French fries at Friendly's
- The Cushman Bakery truck making home deliveries

- Cream and peas on toast
- Ice cream with jimmies at the Dairy Twist
- Eating donuts in the shop at the end of Grove Ave

- Chef Boyardee Spaghettios family size can. Early child abuse.
- Sunning on an old beach

towel at Town Beach waiting for the ice cream truck●Mancini's jojo potatoes

●Filling the little brown paper bags with penny candy●Midnight trips to Jack-In-The-Box●Black raspberry ice cream cone at Tat's

> The restaurant next to Fred Cain's car dealership was called Parker's. My brother and I used to make the hot dog holders and French fries holders for them. They would give us ice cream or fries to take home.--Lorraine Dineen

●Going to Big Joe's for meat pies●Drinking the god awful cocoa from the vending machine at the old rinks●Superman lunchbox packed with a PB&J sandwich, an apple, two cookies, and a small thermos of milk

●Dogs stealing ice cream from the kids at the ice cream truck●Vanilla Cokes●Buying one-cent red fish at Tattersall's

●"Take it" or "Leave it" supper choices
●Coffee and breakfast at Pewter Pot●Saturday suppa: hotdogs, Boston Baked Beans, and warmed brown bread from a can

●2AM tacos at Jack-In-The-Box●Wednesday, Prince Spaghetti Day ●Walking to the

Pharmacy in the Center and getting a hot fudge sundae with marshmallow

•Stop and Go's onion rings•Ten for a dollar hamburgers at Jack-In-The-Box•Friendly's Fribbles•99 cents for a bucket of spaghetti at Rocco's and the all-you-can-eat Fish Fry for $1.99

> We lived on McDonald Road and we had Harold the Candy Man who used to come and park in one of the neighbors' driveway around four o'clock every day. He had a brown station wagon that was packed with junk food! Candy, donuts, sodas, cakes, etc. We thought it was great back then. Now, I think back and would say it's kind of creepy!—Janet Wesinger Moro

•Going out for fried clams•Walking up to Big Joe's Sub Shop for a sub, and a lime rickey at Woodside's soda fountain•Friendly's Swiss Chocolate Almond Sundae

•Tying a rope to our lunch bags and eating lunch in the tree with my friend•Jiffy cookies •Lobster rolls to die for •Mom bringing a tin of hot fried dough to us kids skating on the back swamp

Poole's Bakery
(1960 or so)

by Brent Clark

It was early Saturday morning when I shook my little brother's shoulder again. He was sleeping and always wakes up slow.

"If you don't wake up right now I'm going to leave without you!" I said for the second time.

"Where you goin?" he asked.

"I'm going up town to Poole's to get some bread for Ma."

"Pooles? Why didn't you say so?" he yelled out as he jumped out of bed. I noticed he slept in his clothes again. When you live in a big family of ten kids you can get away with things like that.

We run down the stairs from the attic as quietly as two young boys can. Two sets of stairs and outside in the blink of an eye. We call our dog, cross the street, and head up the sidewalk. The old concrete sidewalk runs all the way up town. My brother avoids the sidewalk because he doesn't like all the rules you have to follow. I myself have holes on the bottom of my sneakers so I stick to the cement. I can't step on the crack or I'll break my mother's back!

Also, whenever there is a bronze plaque in the sidewalk I have to jump, touch it with one foot and yell 'ding-a-ling' as I make my way to the next block. If I don't, then I don't quite know what will happen, but it won't be good!

As we pass a group of houses on the right I look over to the first house on the right and see Richard. Richard Cornish is an older guy who has polio. He is always out in his yard in his wheelchair. I yell out a big "Hi Richard" as we pass by. Sometimes I go visit him, but not today because I'm on a mission.

Then, as I look over the other side of the street I see Attorney Alan Altman's house. His back yard has a giant hedge that is the home-run fence for Rice's Field where we play baseball for countless hours. If you hit a home-run over his hedge then the ball will be lost because everyone is afraid to go get it or ask for it.

On the right is Old Mr. Lewis' house. He has the coolest yard. All along the driveway he has those colored glass things that are on the old poles beside the railroad tracks. He has a ton of them. I yell, "Hi Mr. Lewis!" as we go by. Mr. Lewis waves. "Hi kids!" He is real old and loves his plants and stuff.

As I look down at the sidewalk I remember to watch out for the cracks. I have to take a big step and then a quick shuffle step and another big step. You get used to it after a while. Meanwhile my little brother is walking with one foot on the curb and one foot on the street below. His body goes up with a bob and down, his feet going step-bob-slap, step-bob-slap. He is singing a song. "Lou-Lou skip to my Lou, Lou-Lou skip to my Lou, skip to my Lou my darlin!" He sings with his face up toward the sky, his head and glasses are swinging from side to side. Step, bob, slap, song, head swaying.

I love this guy, my little brother.

Coming up on the right is the good old four-room Walker School. I attend third grade there with a wonderful older teacher whose name is Mrs. Jordan. I love my school with its giant front steps where the principal rings a huge hand bell to call us in before school and from recess.

As we walk by I think of many things about our school. Like, during recess the girls play on one side of the school and the boys on the other. We play giant kickball and dodge ball games. There is three-cent ice cold milk in small bottles during lunch, Manila paper, giant crayons and pencils.

I love the smell of the white paste we use. I even tried to eat it once because it smelled so edible. Oh boy! And for some reason I love that green flaky stuff the janitor puts down to mop the floors.

Next, we come to the old Rotary Park on the right. They are building a brand new Little League baseball field down in the corner. This work has created huge hills of dirt that we play and climb on. The best game is 'King of the Hill.' In the other corner of the park is the ever exciting and exploratory bog. I am so tempted to run over there. We love the bog. We catch polliwogs, frogs, turtles, kibbies, crayfish, and anything else we can get our hands on.

In the winter we skate and have bonfires on the ice. We also slide down the hill behind the fire station right onto the ice. My older brothers drag a giant toboggan up the hill and we all run and jump and push to get on the toboggan as it heads down hill. What a blast we have, as bodies lie all over the hill when we fall off. The victor is the one who stays on to the end. Never me. Believe me!

Over there, on the other side of the bog, is the old McKenna house. A kid over there is Bobby McKenna. He is my age and can hit a baseball farther than anyone I know. He can also whistle real loud through his teeth. His dungarees have big cuffs on the bottom over PF Flyer high top sneakers.

As we walk past the park it calls out to me to come play, explore and run around. I ignore that call with great effort and stay on my errand.

Next is the fire station and all the fire engines are out front today. The firemen are rolling out and rolling up giant fire hoses. It looks like they just got back from a fire call. I yell out "Hi" to a couple of guys and they yell back "Hi kids!" as one of the firemen blows the horn in the long hook-in-ladder truck. The horn is so loud that we jump a mile and I get goose bumps on my neck and arms.

Inside the fire station is a coke machine where we buy ten-cent ice cold cokes sometimes. And on top of the station is a real loud horn that they blow every day at nine o'clock in the morning and nine o'clock at night. Also, they blow the horn on 'no school' days. All little boys love fire stations and we are no exception.

As we continue on, we walk past the new post office that is all shiny and bright. And then the cool little red brick building. It has a cool bronze plaque at the doorway that has a bell on it and says, Bell Telephone. I just have to run up and touch it.

Our pace naturally quickens as we head up the hill to good old Wilmington Center. Across the street I see Church Street Hardware Store where Mr. Griffin is the owner there. He has always been kind to us kids. Even when we bring in dirty and scratched return bottles he acts like we are bringing him a great treasure. After he pays us our deposit money he gives us a Tootsie Roll Pop as we head out the door.

His store is one of my favorite places, with the old creaky wood floors and a giant spinning thing that holds all kinds of nails. Nails are sold by the pound and handed to you in a crinkly brown bag. Most boys will tell you that they love hardware stores with all the cool tools and stuff in them.

As we continue to climb the hill, I stick my hand out and drag my finger along the cement grout between the bricks. The idea is to keep your finger on the grout until you are up and around the corner.

When we round the corner, Poole's Bakery comes into sight. It is at the bottom of the hill, across the street. The store looks like some kind of magical, beautiful, shiny gem as the large plate glass windows reflect the morning sun.

"Poole's!!" My brother yells as he takes off. "Last one there is a rotten egg!"

"FLASH!" I yell as I chase after him. Flash is a favorite comic character who wears a red costume with lightning on his hood. He is one of the fastest of all the legendary super-hero characters.

As we run, our feet hardly touch the ground because we are so young and so light. It's as if we both have the gift of flight because our hearts are in an imaginary world.

My brother hits the door with a bang. He yells tauntingly, "I win, I win, you're a rotten egg!"

Of course I get him with the old "I know you are but what am I?"

As we open the door the smell of baking bread and donuts hits our noses. What a heavenly smell. It smells like warmth, comfort, home, and joy all in one. My stomach growls as we yell out, "Hi Mr. Poole!!"

"Hi boys!" he yelled out.

Mr. Poole is an older, grampy, friendly type of guy. He wears a big white apron, granny glasses, and has a bald head with a little white hair on the sides. His skin is white from baking flour on his arms. I love good old Mr. Poole who has always been kind to us.

"What'll it be today?" he asks as I hand him a note.

As he reads the note he reaches into the glass cabinet in front of us and takes out two beautiful loaves of golden fresh baked bread. He wraps them in crispy wax paper and puts them in a brown paper bag that is just the right size. Then he grabs a flat piece of thin cardboard and folds it into the shape of a box. He then proceeds to put a mix of delicious, fresh baked donuts into it.

As he is doing this I say, "Mr. Poole, the note says only two loaves of bread."

He gives me a glance over his granny glasses and says, "Don't you think I can read, young man?" as he continues to fill the box and close the flap. He grabs the end of a spool of white string and quickly wraps the box with a criss-cross, criss-cross, and breaks the string.

As I hand him a dollar I'm thinking, I'm in big trouble now. My mother only wanted two loaves of bread and she told me to bring back the change. I quickly do the math in my head, two loaves of bread at 27 cents a loaf equals 54 cents. I need to bring home 46 cents or I am in deep trouble.

After a ring of the bell and the slam of the drawer, I hear the sound of change clinking as he hands me 46 cents with a smile. "The donuts are on the house boys!"

"Thank you Mr. Poole. Thanks!" I yell as I hand the free donuts to my surprised little brother. Then with huge smiles we head for the door.

"Oh, boys. Wait!" He yelled excitedly as he grabbed little pieces of wax paper and grabbed a jelly donut for each one of us and says, "One for the road!"

My heart is so full. I can't believe how nice this man is to us as I take a bite of the donut right where the hole is, because you have to follow certain rules you know.

As we head back up the hill I see Ames News Store, Joe Ryan's Barber Shop where we get our whiffle haircuts, and Wilmington Center Pharmacy that has a real soda fountain.

Turning the corner at the top of the hill we head toward home. My brother starts singing "Lou-Lou, skip to my Lou!" I lock arms with him and we skip with that goofy skip-hop-skip-hop way that boys do that just can't get the skipping thing down.

(Copyright Brent Clark, 2016)

Our Early Years

Story shared by Sandra Wilson

I remember the summer cottage we lived in on Cedar Street in Wilmington. It was around 1947. We had just moved from Woburn when my parents bought the small house. I was only about two years old then but I still remember some things in those early years.

The little house had only three rooms. We also had an outhouse in the corner of the backyard since the cottage didn't even have a bathroom. There was also no electricity and no running water, like a rustic cabin in the woods. My mom was pregnant with my brother Stephen.

I used to go with dad to help carry water back to the house. We walked up Cedars to the end of Harris Road. There was a tall water faucet sticking out the ground. We filled our jugs to the top with pure, clean water, then trekked back to the house. We had to do this every single day.

I also remember my dad, mom, and me standing on a square heat grate in the floor to stay warm when it was cold. The house at first had coal heat, but later when it was remodeled dad had it converted to oil heat.

In those days I remember mom had the milkman deliver quarts of fresh milk early in the mornings. The bread man also came to our house with baked goods and delicious breads. Every time we kids saw him we would run to his truck. Mom would get her bread, and me and dad would get a donut. Mom also had the Fuller Brush man come to the house to sell his goods, as well as the Watkins man. It was so routine, people coming to our house selling things.

Eventually the outhouse came down because we finally had a real indoor bathroom. No more cold mornings running to the backyard. That three room cottage had been transformed into a three bedroom home with a dining room, one bath, and a walk down a few steps into the living room from the kitchen.

All the kids in the neighborhood loved to go sledding in the winter after a good old New England snowstorm. We used to slide down the snow covered street or down the neighbor's hilly yard. Our parents never had to worry about where we were or what we were doing. When the street lights came on we knew it was time to go home. Kids felt safe and well protected in those days. And you couldn't have asked for a more then friendly police department.

In those days back in Wilmington, neighbors helped each other and watched over the nearby families. At cookouts, neighbors would just drop in, and that was okay. I remember we could walk into our friends' houses without knocking and we never felt threatened or got yelled at. We were welcomed any time.

I left high school in 1961 when it was still a combined junior high and high school. I took a visit back to Wilmington twenty years later. Things had changed, as they always do. I had some good memories growing up there, even during the hard times.

There's one rather strange, but newsworthy story I remember from those early days. There was a car accident in town, and as far as I can remember a man didn't survive. At that time there was no hospital in Wilmington, so the ambulance had to drive to Wakefield.

Well, so the story goes, the ambulance driver in no real rush since his victim was already gone, decided to stop at a little grocery store on his way out of town. He went inside to get a soda for himself and his partner.

While he was inside, his partner saw a hitch-hiker on the side of the road and offered him a ride. He decided they could drop the fellow off en-route. The hitch-hiker jumped in the back.

Apparently the partner forgot to inform the driver of their new passenger. When they got close to where the rider wanted to be let out, the driver felt a hand on his shoulder and heard a man say, "You can drop me off here."

You can imagine what happened next. The ambulance went off the road and the driver leaped out and took off running. His partner told the police the driver probably thought the dead body had came back to life. Well, the driver quit the next day.

Wilmington had its own personality back in those days, but it was wonderful growing up there.

Life on Butters Row

By Tony Kissel

I came to Wilmington in 1961 after spending five years in an orphanage in Roxbury, Massachusetts. The place was nicknamed 'The Home', and we were taught by Franciscan nuns who demanded obedience at all times. Locked iron gates surrounded 'The Home' and separated us from a normal childhood and kids from the neighborhood.

My father remarried and we bought a small bungalow on Butters Row with one and a half acres of woods. To me it was paradise. I picked blueberries, ice skated in the backyard during the winter, and climbed the pine tree outside the back door. I walked up to Chestnut Street to take the school bus to the Boutwell School where I entered the sixth grade.

I recall standing at the bus stop one day and all of us were looking up in the sky for Russian missiles that were expected to be heading our way. School was a blast for me after my previous experience. Mrs. Rogers was my teacher. She was firm but fair, and lost her husband during the school year. We all cried when she came back to school.

My favorite memory was the day she picked up a boy by his shirt collar and hung him up on the coat rack right outside the classroom door. Everybody laughed at him as he swayed back and forth, and he didn't dare try to get down.

At recess a few boys played marbles and some of us played tackle football and tackled whoever had the ball. I remember losing the annual school spelling bee to Diane Houle. The word I misspelled was lavatory. I had never heard of it before.

I tried out for Little League baseball at age eleven with no prior experience. The Indians drafted me, probably because Charles Malatesta, the assistant coach, was my next-door neighbor. I stunk at first because I had to learn how to throw, catch, and hit. Coach Eddie Sullivan was strict, and our wool uniforms were hot in the sweltering heat. I played in right field and had the good fortune to watch our two great pitchers Whitey and Oakie (Donnie White and Danny O'Connell) win game after game for us.

In our second season we finished in first place, and our sponsor, Chisholm Mink Farm, threw a great party for us that included a tour of their mink farm. At the Little League banquet a young Carl Yastrzemski of the Red Sox spoke to us about growing up on a potato farm in Long Island and then attending Notre Dame. I idolized him because I'm part Polish (although he ruined my batting average because I tried to copy his swing but couldn't).

There weren't any other organized youth sports besides Little League, so the boys in the neighborhood organized our own activities. The Chestnut Hill skating rink became our hockey arena. I had never ice skated before, so naturally I stunk at first as I tried to keep up with the other players.

Bobby Capozzi and I were the two youngest boys, so we were always the last picks in every sport. We built fires in trash cans to huddle by to keep warm. I recall walking home after dark and so frozen that my ice skates were still on and my two outstretched hands held my gear in them.

During the Eastern Winter Olympics Speed Skating Trials held at the Chestnut Street skating rink I watched Jeanne Ashworth lap the entire field to qualify for the Winter Olympics! She was one of my first heroes, and I rooted for her on television in the Olympics.

One Christmas morning my parents gave me an English Raleigh bicycle. The other boys owned Schwinns and tried to help me learn how to ride a bike that spring, but grew impatient with me. One day I pedaled by myself and a few seconds later realized I had finally gotten the hang of it.

You always knew where the boys in the neighborhood were by where our bikes were parked. They were seldom parked though, as we usually just left them lying on their sides on the ground. We followed Indian trails in the woods around Butters Row. I imagined what life was like before the first Butters family set foot in the area.

Someone told me that a large stone structure in the middle of a stream was where an Indian chief was buried. We did what many boys did back then: had acorn fights, played whiffle ball, jumped off garage roofs, built a tree house in the woods, or played tackle football against other neighborhoods. I respected the older boys and learned a lot from them. They accepted me even though I stunk, and they were excellent role models too. I am not sure if they knew about my background.

When my parents split up they sold the house and I moved with my father first to Tewksbury, and later to Somerville where I graduated. I didn't have that same feeling that I had when I lived in Wilmington.

A few decades later the small town of Homer, NY brought back fond memories of my childhood years. When coaching my son's Little League championship team I recalled forty years earlier my own feelings as a carefree twelve-year old. Some towns have it, and you know the feeling that you get.

It's called Home.

> **Remember when...**
>   ...you woke up early Christmas morning
>   and on the kitchen table the glass of milk
>   was half empty and the cookies were gone.
>   You believed!

A Thanksgiving Memory

Story contributed by
Debbie Harrington

Having grown up on Grove Ave, many of my memories include spending time at Silver Lake across my street. Swimming in the summer. Skating in the winter. My grandmother yelling at me to put my coat back on. She would catch me every time in my first through fourth grade years walking to the Mildred H. Rogers School up on the beach, no matter the weather.

And, the Betterment Hall. While many may remember going to church there, I do not.

I remember the Betterment Hall for other reasons. The Boy Scouts held their meetings there and a lady's group met there as well.

The first things I recall were the dances held in the Hall on weekends. My dad would climb a ladder and aim a bright flashlight for the spotlight dances. I was only eleven or twelve, but it was also where a boy asked me to dance for the very first time.

The second memory, and my favorite one, was our family Thanksgiving dinners at the Hall. My grandparents also lived on Grove Ave, and many years would have the whole family over for the holiday feast. Our huge family would fill much of the building.

At dinner were Mom's five sisters and six brothers, all married and with growing families of their own, plus our great-grandmother, as well as grandma's sister and husband. Grandma and our moms did all the cooking and after the terrific dinner Mom and all my aunts cleaned up.

We, the grandkids, provided entertainment for the relaxed and stuffed crowd. A few of my cousins were quite talented, but others, well not so much. But we all did some sort of silly skit and had lots of fun. And Santa! Can't forget Santa who arrived with a present for each of the grandkids.

I can still remember my Dad and my uncles sitting around a big table smoking cigarettes and playing cards.

Years later when we stopped having Thanksgiving at Betterment Hall, there were thirty-five grandchildren. That was when my dear great-grandma passed.

Thanksgiving in those days was the best.

The Richard Welch Memorial
Fallen Heroes: Part I

by Fred Shine

Richard W. Welch served with the 173rd Airborne Brigade and was killed in action on September 13th 1968, in Vietnam. He was awarded the Silver Star posthumously for bravery in combat while defending his unit from overwhelming enemy forces. He was a 1967 graduate of Wilmington High School.

When I decided to build Richard's monument I wanted it to be something 'special,' something that would honor both his family and other veterans. I did not want the traditional 'street corner sign' as seen in many small towns. I wanted something that had true meaning.

When I started looking, I got flack from people right away, still wanting to forget the Vietnam War and not wanting any monuments. I knew funding for the project would be difficult.

I had some supporting allies in town. Representative Jim Miceli was behind me from the start. Mr. Downs from the Highway Dept. and Selectman Mike Ciara, who also graduated with Richard and me, and a friend of Millie Welch, Mrs. Fullerton, whose son John. J. Fullerton, Jr., was also killed in the war. At the time Mrs. Fullerton had no idea I had plans to erect a monument for her son as well.

I found a suitable site I thought would be pretty special. At the corner of Main Street and Bridge Lane sat a little wooded island. It was a spot where 'The Rat Traps' would hang out and whistle at girls driving by and harass kids like me who did not fit into their rowdy group

The spot was also at the base of the new Fred F. Cain Bridge, and would be an appropriate slap in the face to the town and state for what they had done in naming the structure. It was the perfect location, but the plot was state owned.

I went to Jim Miceli who tried for years to get me permission to build the monument there, and even proposed a bill to dedicate the site for the memorial. But it kept getting delayed.

An old friend of mine, Mike Mucci, who was a State Trooper and personal bodyguard for Massachusetts Governor Ed King, helped me out. I told Mike I wanted to meet the Governor and he arranged the meeting. In Boston, Governor King said to me, "Don't wait for the House to vote on your request. Just do it. No one is going to stop you!" I asked if he would dedicate the monument when it went up and he said, "Absolutely!"

Mr. Downs was told I had permission to proceed, and he had the highway crew start clearing the spot. David Welch, Richard's brother, owned a foundation company and donated the base for the monument. Mr. Downs was able to get four beautiful pieces of granite which were used in the old Jenks Bridge being demolished.

The granite was hand-forged in Wilmington back in the 1800s, so it was also part of the town's history. I ordered the bronze plaque and raised enough money to both build the monument and also hold a lunch for anyone who attended. Rocco Depasquale (Rocco's Restaurant owner and also one of my strongest supporters on the Board of Selectmen), offered to host a pre-dedication coffee and pastry breakfast at his expense.

Members of the VFW were to be the Honor Guard. Things were finally coming together and a dedication date was set. A couple weeks before the dedication, things started to fall apart. Ed King, the Governor, had already confirmed his attendance and needed a clearance for his helicopter to land across from the Police Station. That was an easy problem, but there was still a lot of local resentment toward Vietnam vets, and I was running into trouble at several turns.

The VFW refused to send an Honor Guard. The plaque manufacturer went on strike. It appeared that this thing wasn't going to happen. But fighting in Vietnam changed me. I had been bullied in school, but I was stronger now and I would not give up.

I had a temporary copper plaque made up and affixed to the monument in time for the ceremony. I called a nearby U.S. Army post and explained the situation about being denied honor guards from the local VFW. In no uncertain terms the Army rep said they would be there. Jim Miceli, Mike Caira, and U.S. Senator Bob Bull would also be there.

But more important to me, Millie, Dave, Richard's sisters, the Rat Traps, Mrs. Fullerton and her entire family and friends would be there as well. The Governor showed up and the dedication was covered by WBZ-TV. Despite all the obstacles, my vision of a memorial for Richard Welch had become a reality. Millie was proud. Hell, I was proud.

But, something strange happened right after the ceremony. Dave, Richard's brother who had been one of my tormentors back in school, approached me and said, "I don't understand it! After all the years we picked on you, beat you up, and bullied you, YOU went and paid tribute to my brother!"

I simply told him Richard was MY brother too! We've been friends ever since, and David donated all the footings to all the monuments. David died of a massive heart attack while at lunch a few years ago.

However, the BEST thing that happened was the U.S. Army Honor Guard's captain's comment after the dedication. With tears in his eyes he told

75

me they had participated in many memorial ceremonies.

This one was special to them since they were from the 173rd Airborne Brigade and it was the first time they were on site to honor one of their own. The captain vowed that the group would be available for any other dedications I needed them for. That was special to me too!

Olympic Medal Winner

Submitted by Frank Stone

Over the many years Wilmington has had its share of accomplished citizens. From business owners to educators to first responders to civil servants to military members to local athletes, our small town has nurtured a number of admirable, even inspirational people.

One notable person is Jeanne Ashworth from the WHS class of 1956, and she was my classmate. She was a talented athlete in several high school sports, but her passion was devoted to ice speed skating. She learned to skate on area ponds as a young girl growing up in Wilmington.

Her parents, who owned and operated the popular Sunnyhurst Ice Cream shop up on Route 129, supported their daughter's dream to compete. When she was only ten years old she had competed in the Silver Skates event at Boston Garden.

In 1960, for the first time, women were allowed to participate in the Winter Olympics speed skating races, which up until that time had been a male sport. Against tough competition Jeanne won a bronze medal in the 500 meter (nearly a third of a mile distance) at the Squaw Valley, California contest.

Jeanne was the only American woman to ever earn a coveted Olympics medal in speed skating. And, I might add, she is the only one from Wilmington to have won an Olympic medal.

For years later, Jeanne continued to skate and compete. In total, she had won eleven national speed skating championships. She also raced in consecutive 1964 and 1968 Winter Olympics, and in 1980 she went to the Olympics as a delegate from the USA.

In her later years the medal winner continued to train upcoming Olympic speed skaters. To top off her fabulous career, Jeanne Ashworth was inducted into the Lake Placid Hall of Fame in 1993.

Wilmington, Massachusetts, is indeed honored to call this superb athlete a past resident of our quaint town.

Places We Went

Wilmington Residents

Compared to the cities where many of us growing up in Wilmington came from, our town was limited in places to go. Or was it? We not only remember the stores and shops and restaurants in the area, but perhaps more importantly perhaps, we have great memories of the 'other' places where we spent much of our youth. Let's take a peek into the past as expressed by town residents and smile a bit.

- Retrieving golf balls from the ponds at the Garden of Eden golf course and reselling them
- Going to the Friday night discos at K of C
- Renting wooden rowboats at McQuades Beach

- Getting off the train after shopping in Boston and stopping at Poole's Bakery on the way home
- Concerts on the Common
- Eli's Country Store in North Wilmington

- Going to the Starlight Drive-In movie in North Reading
- Eating at Kitty's the night before Thanksgiving
- Finding a booth at Friendly's after a football game

> When you got your first car and needed new tires, you'd go to McNamara Tire. You'd tell Mr. McNamara, with his bushy eyebrows, about whatever problem there was and he'd always give you the same line. "Yeah, yeah, yeah, we'll have to check the nut behind the wheel!"

- Painting the apple red on the Baldwin Apple monument one Halloween•Looking at the pictures of service men hanging on the walls inside Huntley's Diner•Camp 40 Acres

- Going out to the beach at the lake and yelling "Shark!" right after the Jaws movie came out•Parties at the old rink on Ballardvale•Going to the movies above Wilton's Furniture

- Ricky's Dog House•Someone losing their front teeth during a kickball game on Pilling Road•A new BB gun and the grumpy old neighbor's window

- Trying to figure a way out of Hathaway Acres your first time there•The Tewksbury Wamesit Drive-In•25¢ boys regular haircuts at O'Briens Barber Shop

- Dropping a quarter in St. Dorothy's offering basket•High School study period at Pewter Pot•Saturday night Coffee House at the Congregational Church

- Watching the fireworks from the grass in Wakefield•Four boys, one bathroom, and a very long wait•The rumble of the loose wooden planks as cars drove over the railroad bridges

●Mancini's menu written on paper plates●Big Joe's●Getting a certificate from Dr. Wallent the dentist to get an ice cream cone at Harry's Drugstore in North Wilmington

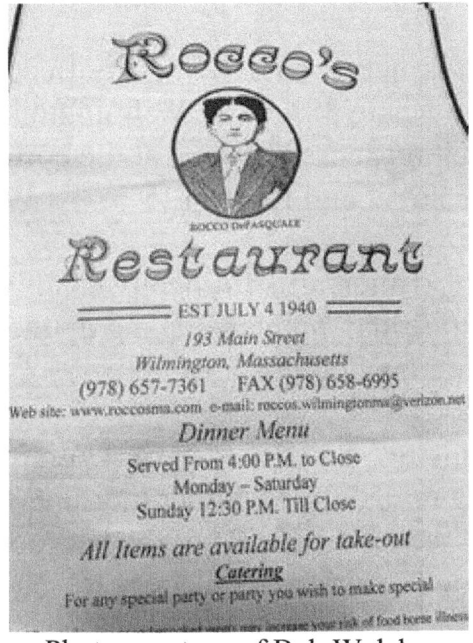

Photo courtesy of Bob Welch

●Breakfast at Stelio's●Walking to Sweetheart Plastic from the high school to work●Learning to bowl at the Wilmington Bowling Alley with its groove down the middle of the lanes

●Going to Lucci's when it was just a house on the corner●Simon's Department Store● Picking peppers at Scharappa's Farm in North

Wilmington during a frost forecast

•Weinberg's giant pumpkins•May Day processions at St. Dorothy's•Having to honk the horn on the Butters Row Bridge and listen for the return horn from the other side

•The Bookmobile parked at Baby Beach•The arcade on Route 38•North Wilmington horse shows behind Jensen's Farm at the corner of Andover Street and Route 125

•Going to Tattersall's for penny candy•CYO dances on Friday nights•Picking up the latest 45s at Grants•Coombs Furniture

•The minstrel shows held at St. Dorothy's
•Waking up on a cold winter morning seeing layers of ice on the inside of the bedroom windows•The rides at Salisbury Beach

•The Yum Yum Shop•The best selection of Archie comic books at Weinberg's•People coming from all over for the awesome subs at Farmer and the Dell

•Frozen laundry hanging on the line•Ernie's Super Gas•Sitting on the Buzzell School hill on a spring night drinking beer with friends

•Sunday morning and Poole's Bakery jelly

donuts!•Pinehurst Drive-In•Stopping at Sunnyhurst for ice cream cones on our way home from the beach

•Slamming of the front porch screen door
•The mink farm•Friends getting change to buy enough gas to hit Hampton Beach

•Going to the old auction barn at the Wilmington/Tewksbury line•Turtle Pond beside the old high school on Adam Street

1936 Wilmington Theatre movie program
Photo courtesy of:
Alice (Chisholm) Shaffer WHS Class of 1963

Weinberg's

By Larz Neilson

Do you remember Weinberg's? In the 1950s it was Wilmington's best clothing store. Oh, yeah, it was the only one.

Morris Weinberg started selling clothing door-to-door in Wilmington in the 1920s. He then built a retail store in Wilmington Square, next to the theater.

The store that everyone remembers was built in the very early 1950s by Myer "Mike" Weinberg, son of Morris. In addition to great clothing lines, Weinberg's also sold ice skates. At the time Wilmington had a skating club that was considered "home of champions."

The store sold a lot of speed skates. Mike Weinberg was president of the Wilmington Skating Club. His wife Crysille worked alongside him in many capacities. The Weinbergs were solid supporters of the community, helping in many ways.

The Wilmington Skating Club taught local youngsters that they could become champions. Two women, Janet Backman and Jeanne Ashworth, were at the top of their class, true North American skating champions.

The Weinberg children, Mike Jr. and Nancy, were also consistent winners on the ice. Nancy started in the "Pee Wee" group and moved up, winning championships at every level. Mike became a world champion barrel jumper in the junior bracket.

Weinberg's store at the corner of Main Street and Middlesex Avenue was the most popular store in town at the time. Mike added onto it twice as the business grew and thrived. Things went well until about 1960.

In 1959 DeMoulas built a supermarket a half mile down the road. It was the beginning of what later became a popular shopping center. One of the first new tenants was a discount store, Simon's.

Weinberg's had always sold good quality clothing, but Simon's cut into their sales. Mike Weinberg tried to compete on price. He first went with cheaper clothes, and eventually brought in other low-price goods. But, it was Simon's game, and it had a bigger, glitzier store.

As time went on, Mike began selling penny candy, and ironically, that is what the store is best remembered for now. He also had a table of paperback books with no covers, selling for a dime each. There were few racks of clothes left since he had lost many of the good lines he once carried.

In the 1970s, Mike subdivided the building, renting out one side to Cumberland Farms convenience store. The legendary clothing, ice skating equipment, and penny candy store came to a sad end by the late 1970s.

Loyal customers and close friends saw Mike endure a long bout with cancer. Crysille cared for him during his struggle. Then, as life would have it, she was killed in a traffic accident caused by a drunk driver. Mike died only a few months later.

My Neighborhood
By Tony Meads

Like many others from Wilmington, I have a boatload of great memories growing up there. A lot of them are times with my friend, Steve Johnson, Bob's younger brother.

I remember we used to float around in the big swamp behind the Moore's house. We had an old 1940s or 1950s car hood with its curved sides as our primitive boat. The swamp was next to the dirt road that one of the neighborhood boys, Ralph Van Steensburg, lived on.

Steve and I would use a long stick to push our wobbly hood-boat around all the nooks and crannies of the weed and thicket entangled swamp. We always needed two of us to survive the dangerous cruise. One kid would push the tipsy steel raft with the stick, many times getting it stuck in the thick bottom sludge. The other would bail water that kept seeping into the old bucket. We couldn't have been much more then seven or eight years old.

I remember my mother would warn me about the swamp. She said there was quicksand there, probably trying to keep me from coming home all wet and muddy. But that just seemed to make the adventure even better.

I also remember floating along the edge of Silver Lake in the same manner, but on chunks of ice in the spring time when the solid ice was melting and breaking up. Again, Steve and I would each have a stick to push us along the lake's banks from what was called 'Baby Beach' near Route 38 over toward the school by Town Beach.

We did our best balancing ourselves on the ice packs from opposite ends. Otherwise, one end would tip up or dip down into the cold water and we'd slide off, which would end up in a not too pleasant situation when we got home. At least at my house.

I remember on those summer days there wasn't much car traffic on Main Street back then.

I could hear the muffled sounds of people way down at the lake from my own backyard, which I'm guessing was a couple miles away. There could be a half hour without a car driving by and the lake noise always filled the air.

Also, I remember walking from Fuller's Beach near the Grove Ave curve, all the way to Tat's to buy some penny candy or a Popsicle. The road and sidewalk would be so hot on our bare feet. We would have to run from one sandy spot or grassy growth growing out of the sidewalk cracks to keep our feet from burning.

Steve, Billy Gray, and I would get up early in the summer mornings while it was still dark. We'd take kerosene lanterns and our simple tackle gear, walk to the lake and go fishing. We'd watch the sunrise as we fished in the quiet, still water.

Some nights my friends and I would take turns sleeping out in each other's backyards. Sometimes we would pool the little money we had and make a trip to Dunkin' Donuts at midnight, or maybe even two in the morning. Dunks was new in town and open 24/7, so the temptation was too much to resist.

I remember one time when my brother Rob and his friend Tommy went fishing at the lake. Well, Tommy took one last cast of his line and hooked Rob in the head. They took a pair of wire cutters and simply snipped the top half of the hook off.

Rob had that bump from the imbedded piece of hook in his head until the day he died. For some reason that was one of those things that you just didn't tell your parents about. Probably because they would be really pissed that there would be a doctor's bill involved. Especially in those days, when the doctor used to come to your house when you were sick.

I could go on and on about our tree huts in the woods and our dug-out underground forts and the Tarzan swings we rigged to tall trees. I could gladly share stories about walking to the lake shore along the stretch of road from Ernie's Gas Station up Main Street. We'd collect discarded soda bottles on the road side and in the creek to cash them in at Tat's for a few pennies, then go over to the penny candy counter.

As a matter of fact, I still have an old gas pump from Ernie's station that my brother Rob was going to restore as a memory in front of his garage.

Those were good days.

Remember when...we hid out in the woods behind the football field after skipping school, hoping the truant officer wouldn't find us

A Long Hike to Silver Lake

By Brent Clark

Telling about the 'olden days' wouldn't be complete without describing a day at good old Silver Lake in the 1960s.

We often walked, rode our bikes, or ran to the lake when we were as young as seven and eight years old. The lake was a few miles from where we lived at 99 Church Street, and then a little later at 23 Floradale Ave.

Our long trip to the lake would begin across the street on Central Street. The Fritags lived on the corner. They were a large family of mostly boys who we often battled with throughout the days until they moved away. Mrs. Fritag was a wonderful lady who was frequently kind to me. I always remember the folks who were nice to me back then.

At the end of Central lived the Breens on the right corner, and the Stones on the left corner. Both families had kids our age and we played together on occasion. From there we would go left on Middlesex Avenue in our journey.

Just up the way we would take a right on Clark Street. On the corner there was an old house that we were always talking and wondering about. It was a mysterious place to us kids. There was something about that old house that caught our interest. I believe it had been a store or inn at one time.

Then, farther up on Clark Street—just before the railroad tracks—was good old Doc Fagan's house on the right. He ran his office in his house and many of my friends got patched up with all kinds of injuries at his house. Doc Fagan went on to be the high school football team doctor, if I remember correctly.

Just over the tracks was Railroad Avenue. When I was older I had tried to hop a freight train on those tracks. Everything was going fine as I ran alongside the moving train, but as I reached up to grab the metal rung, the train seemed to speed up. I took some pretty good lumps as I flew into the rocks and picker bushes. I lied to my girlfriend at the time and told her I had gotten into a fight and she should've seen the other guy.

The Gardners and Hembrees lived there on Railroad Avenue. Butchie Hembree was in my classes all through school. He could kick a kickball a mile in those giant kickball games we used to have at the old Walker School just up the street.

Soon we'd come to the end of Clark Street at the intersection of Main Street (Rt. 38). Just on the right there was an old house on a hill with a huge garden in the backyard. The owner was always working outside on his flowers and vegetables. Although we didn't know him, we always waved to the old guy with a big "Hello!"

Continuing our walk, after the turn on the left was a bridge over the tracks, which is now just a walking bridge. Route 129 went up that way in the old days, and not by Rocco's restaurant.

There used to be a penny candy store in a yellow house just over the bridge. I can't remember what was on the left, but the spot later became the Pewter Pot muffin house. But, on the right was Elfman's Office, and across from that was the Gardner Building. (My dad actually lived in an apartment up there from 1963 on, and the place is still there.)

I know this is going to be hard to believe, but next was Wilmington Plaza. At the time DeMoulas supermarket and Simon's department store were there, but nothing else—no kidding. And across the street the large piece of land, the location of Wilmington Ford, which is now a plaza, was only woods—just woods. Actually, as kids those dense woods were kinda scary and we always went by them in a hurry.

Then we came up on the good old Jenny Gas Station owned by the Bridges. (We used to call the older man Louie and his son Jake.) My oldest brother Doug, my other brother Stan, and Johnny Poloian worked there at times. My old schoolmate Ralph Block used to hang out there. Louie and Jake were always kind to me as I frequently pulled my junk box cars in there as a teenager to be worked on, generally on the cheap.

Behind the gas station was Wilmington Transmission, owned by Mr. Fortunata. I think he was the older brother of a neighborhood kid named Anthony that my brothers used to play with. We used to slingshot grape fights, and that kid was always a riot to us little kids. He was very excitable and yelled out with a lisp when us little kids 'ambushed' him.

Beside that place was good old McNamara Tire Company. Mr. McNamara had the biggest, bushiest eyebrows I have ever seen in my life. I remember two of his sons, Steve and Mike, who worked there. It was another place I visited frequently when I grew older.

Next in our travel was a famous restaurant and landmark on the left, Rocco's. They had the greatest Italian food. On the right as we still traveled toward the lake is Harvard Avenue where I rented a converted garage from the Peters family when I got married.

Wilmington Diner was farther down Main Street. It had the best hotdogs on the planet. My dad used to get us a hotdog sometimes when we all worked for him on one of the houses he was building. Those hotdogs were buttered and fried, then wrapped in wax paper. Maybe those dogs tasted so good because my dad bought them for us.

More woods lined the road as we passed some kind of gas station on the left. On the right side was a one story white building that was set back, and I think it was used for dances. Then, I believe St. Dorothy's Catholic Church was built.

Oh—my—gosh!

The most famous place in every kid's heart was Tattersall's penny candy store. I approach this subject and description with great respect and reverence. The front door to the tiny store was a screen door that rang a bell when you entered and slammed when you got inside. There were great lengths of glass display cabinets just loaded with every kind of candy imaginable.

I remember standing there in that cool store and looking up at a tall balding man as he waited patiently with a small crinkly brown bag for me to pick my treasure of candy one piece at a time. Some of the candies were Bulls-eyes and licorice and Fireballs and mint juleps and Bazooka bubble gum and Dots and root beer barrels, and so many more. You could fill a whole bag for a dime or ten pennies.

I remember going inside Tats from the hot summer sun with sand still on my feet from the beach. The wonderful smell of candy and ice cream attacked my nose every time I entered. And I can still hear the sound of that screen door slamming to this day. That store is one of my best memories of my childhood.

Next, we would travel up Grove Avenue toward the public beach. On the right was Silver Lake Paint and Hardware where I purchased Touraine paint (made in Everett, Mass) for my painting company that I had in my teen years. Just a point of interest—my painting company consisted of a ladder strapped to the roof of my old 1963 four-door Chevy Biscayne, and me. The good old days...

Then on the right was the Williams' house just beside Baby Beach, who I hung around with later in life. Baby Beach was forbidden to us kids, but it was awesome and had a large anchored raft. I must confess that when I turned a little older I used to sneak out to the raft and ride a giant alligator log all around the whole lake.

Baby Beach had no lifeguard and a lot of older kids hung out there. Those were the main reasons the beach was off limits to us younger kids.

Up the road a bit along the lake on the right was wild lakefront maintained by no one. If you swam there you had to keep your body up because there were a ton of weeds in the shallows and what we used to call "mucky-guck" if you stood up.

Finally, I would come to my old hanging grounds, the public beach. We would enter through the chain-link gate, show our Silver Lake residence tag, drop our stuff, and run as fast as we could with a kick and a skip and a final dive into the cool water.

After a long afternoon of swimming and jumping and splashing, and having a general all around wonderful time, we would have to hike all the way back home.

I can still see us now in a long, single line with our towels half rolled and dragging behind us. I loved the lake (like most Wilmington kids who had spent any amount of time there).

What I wouldn't give to be a kid again and hang out at good old Silver Lake for just a few days.

Copyright by Brent Clark

Hanging Out & Muscle Cars

By Joe Casey

Back in the late '60s and early '70s there was a group of friends that used to meet nightly in the good weather at what we referred to as 'Sunnyhurst.'

Now, even at that time the dairy, which had also served ice cream and had been a very popular place to meet or gather, had moved on. To us kids it was "meet down at Sunnyhurst at 6:00!"

Most evenings a neat line of cool sports and muscle cars could be seen in the parking lot directly abutting Route 129 across from Avco. Eight or ten cars were usually there, their drivers hanging around and showing off their cool machines. There were Corvettes, a GTO or two, and an assortment of polished cars all shined up and looking fine.

Ed Lord, George Nugent, Jack Strob, Gerry Otis, John Marsi, and John Hall, along with my self were among the regulars. I'd be driving a silver '68 Vette convertible. Next to it would be Ed's '69 green T-top, then Gerry's gold '69 convert, and eventually George's Nashua blue '65 coup. We'd talk about the events of the day, share stories, and generally 'hang out.'

We even had our own nicknames within the group. 'Cakes', 'Alphie', 'Bull', 'Sas', and 'Mars', the origins of each remains a closely guarded secret.

Hanging out at our favorite spot we never caused any trouble and just enjoyed a low-key time amongst friends and classmates. Wilmington Police Officer Bob Shelly would wave when he cruised by us while on his nightly patrol. He knew we were basically good kids, but a frequent drive-by let us know he was there.

It doesn't seem like that was a half century ago, but it was, and is evidenced by the passing of a number of the guys. Years taking its toll. Perhaps some day we'll meet again to catch up.

Remember when...
...you and your friends just drove around town for the fun of it

---

My Wilmington Family

by Cathy (Fantasia) Seely

I believe I was ten years old when my family bought our first house. We were at the time a family of seven. The Fantasias, my Dad Tony, my Mom Lucille, and my siblings, Tony, Skip, Steve, Anna Marie, and myself, Cathy.

I was the oldest girl and third oldest of the group. Up until that point we had moved every single year. To say we were excited about our new house was an understatement.

It was a perfect house on 8 Catherine Ave in North Wilmington. I had always believed that my

Dad bought the house on that street because it had the same name as me, Catherine.

It was a wonderful little ranch style home on a half acre of land, fenced-in yard with two giant weeping willow trees that were so pretty. The neighborhood had many families and other children to become friends with.

My Dad had a great job at DuPont in Everett, and Mom was a stay-at-home Mom. I remember my father painting the trim on that white ranch a lavender, my mother's favorite color. It was different, but it made her happy, and he was happy to do it.

So we began our life in Wilmington with the announcement that my Mom was going to be adding to the family. Not only a baby, but twins!! So, in a very short amount of time we became a family of nine. Michael and Michele would complete the Fantasia family.

I started school that first year at the Swain School, and I was happy to begin making new friends that would still be there after a year. Moving every year certainly had its drawbacks. My second year was at the Glen Road School with Mrs. Roth. I rode the bus to and from school and quickly became friends with Fran McLean. We would hang out together after school and listen to 45s and talk about boys. Life was so carefree.

In May of 1962 the twins turned a year old. I was eleven and my oldest brother Tony was just fifteen. Skip was a year behind him, Steve was probably nine, and Anna Marie was only five.

On July third my Dad suffered a major heart attack. It wasn't his first, but it was pretty bad. Dad was unconscious for about two weeks, and Mom traveled back and forth to the hospital every day to be with him.

Family and neighbors stepped up and made sure those at home were cared for. On July 16 my Dad woke up. Mom called home to let us know she was going to stay at the hospital a little longer. We were all excited for Daddy to be okay.

About six o'clock that evening Dad didn't feel well. Mom thought maybe Dad had just overdone that day. She went to roll down his bed, and when she looked up, Dad had slumped over. She called for help right away. But, there was nothing they could do. Dad's heart just gave out...he was gone. Mom had to come home and tell us the bad news.

I wish I could remember the details of that day and those that followed. I knew we were all devastated and heart broken. The neighborhood rallied around us, as did the rest of the family and friends. My mother was thirty-seven years old with seven children to take care of without our Dad. He died at forty-seven.

That fall I went to the brand new North Intermediate School near our house. I believe the teachers were extra attentive to our family because of what we had gone through. My most vivid memory was Mr. Nolan, my history teacher and guidance counselor.

Mr. Nolan was the one person I could go to and sit in his office and talk to. He encouraged me and listened to me, and I really believe he instilled in me the strength that my dad would have. We were lucky to have moved to a town where so many wonderful people cared for my family.

To say that was a life changing time in my life is an understatement. We all grew up so fast. I loved that town. I graduated and made many good friends there. Sure, we drifted apart, but when times like reunions bring us together, we reconnect like townies do. We reminisce and rekindle those friendships, and as each year ticks by we treasure those who are still part of our circle.

I love my Wilmington High friends, especially the class of 1968. Thank you for being a part of my memories.

Thank you Mr. Nolan. You will never know how much you meant to me.

Thank you for letting me tell my story. Wilmington will always be my hometown.

A Look at Wilmington History

Written by Dianna DiGregorio

We grew up on Church Street when I was little. Our house was across the street from the fire department, which was convenient since my Dad was a fireman. The firemen slept on-site, and as kids we were never allowed in their sleeping quarters. They had a pole that they would slide down from the second floor to the first to get into their gear for an incoming fire call.

At the fire station my Dad used to stock the coke machines. We loved helping him with that job because we always got a free drink out of it. Also, the Humpty Dumpty Potato Chip Company delivered tins of their chips to the firehouse. My Dad always bought a couple of them for our family.

At 9 AM and 9 PM the train whistle would blow, signifying the time of day. You could set your clocks to that whistle. We used to love having our friends over and be outside when it blew because we knew it would scare them—which it always did. Train whistles have been quiet as well. Now it's a quiet town.

There were five of us kids in my family and I was one of the twins. We looked very much alike when we were younger. Sometimes we would switch to confuse people. Our Mom would dress us alike. When we had our class pictures taken at the Walker School they had to re-do our picture as no one could tell us apart. Neither could my Mom. When we got to 5th grade the teachers separated us into different classrooms so we could develop our own personalities.

As kids we were never at home. When we got out of school we would go home, grab our bikes and ride down the street to play with our friends. We would go to the field (what is now known as the Rotary Park) and play baseball, or we would fish in the bog. Most of us used nothing but string and paper clips to catch sunfish. The boys would try and catch the frogs and put firecrackers in their mouths. In the winter we would skate on the bog.

We had a bunch of woods behind our house. We used to walk in there even though it was muddy and swampy. Sometimes we would lose a shoe in the mud. One year we decided to make a haunted trail and charge money for the neighborhood kids to walk through it. We had ghosts hanging in the trees, old dolls that we tied to branches, and other hidden items stuffed in old tree trunks. We pulled discarded bottles from the dump and made smelly witch stews to give our haunted trail more of a creepy factor.

We would also go 'uptown' which was the center where Rte. 62 and Rte. 38 intersect. At one time there was Poole's Bakery, Big Joe's Sandwich Shop, and a variety store. Also, Joe Ryan's barber shop where you could get a crew cut, a whiffle, or a regular cut.

At Woodside Center Pharmacy we would go to the soda fountain and drink Lime Rickey's or get an ice cream. While we were sitting at the counter we would run our fingers under the counter where customers deposited their old pieces of chewing gum. Down the street from the center was Weinberg's Penny Candy Store. That was a fun store for sure.

Recycling back in the day was much different than today. The trash was thrown in the incinerator and burned. Bottles and cans were thrown in the dump (which was the woods behind our house). The food garbage was thrown in a cement container that was buried in the ground. We took turns emptying the garbage and didn't want to look too closely.

To empty it, garbage men would come, lift it out by the handles, and empty it into the open garbage truck. You never wanted to ride your bike behind that truck on a hot and humid day because of the stench.

I went to the Walker School for Grade 1 through Grade 4. I remember the air raid drills we had in our classroom and we had to hide under our desks during the drills. Then I went to the Swain School for 5th grade, which is no longer there. For middle school we were the first to attend the new West Intermediate School, and finished at the Wilmington High School. You had to choose between taking business courses or college courses.

I still shop at DeMoulas—not Market Basket. When people ask me where that is, I know they are not from this area. The DeMoulas store was the anchor for the shopping center. Some of the stores in the plaza were Simon's Department Store, Kings Jewelers, Robert Hall, Friendly's Ice Cream, the Wilmington Pharmacy, Commercial Bank, Grants, and the Clipper Barber Shop.

How things have changed.

"My Dad was friends with Norm Daigle, the manager of DeMoulas, and the Genest Bakery supplier for DeMoulas' driver, Al Swain. Al used to collect the dented cans and out of date bread from the store and bring it to my Dad's gas station. Dad would bring the damaged and expired groceries home and we would take what we wanted. Then we'd put the supplies in our big Radio Flyer wagon and go around to the neighbors and offer the bread and canned foods to those who needed them. What was left we would bring to Charlie Cosgrove to feed his pigs. Our family used to go to Al Swain's house in Londonderry, along with Norm Daigle and his family, to swim in Al's pool. My Dad and I used to meet Norm and Al at Scotty's for coffee or hot chocolate and donuts when we were out plowing snow."

—Terri O'Conners Allum

"When I worked there one of the DeMoulas brothers was the manager. I worked directly for Joe Harrington as a cashier.

"Back then we rang every grocery item up on the register manually. There were no computers, no bar codes, and no scanning.

"Of course there were some customers who carried hand counters to keep track of the total. Boy, if your total didn't match the counter's sum, all the groceries were taken to the office and rung up all over again. I did pretty good, though.

"Most people forgot to add the return deposit required on soda bottles. Also, if the item was priced at two for one and the customer bought

> only one, then an extra penny was added to the order. Today with scanning, that doesn't happen.
>
> "You had better known your math back then too, especially when it came to figuring out the customer's change."
> —Rose Chase

Saving Wilmington Arts
Written by Marjorie Campbell

My mother, Antoinette Campbell, was the mother of nine of us Campbells and was very active in the community. She was also a substitute teacher in all the schools, so people may remember her that way as well.

My mother was an excellent artist and loved to paint and draw. Despite raising all of her children and teaching in the schools, she always fought hard to keep the Arts alive in our schools and in the town of Wilmington.

I remember there were a few times in the '70s and '80s when all of my siblings were going to school, the school district would discuss the need to cut funding. The first classes the schools would try to cut back on were the Arts courses and programs.

My mother would march down to the schools to show up at town meetings to emphasize the importance of a broad curriculum. She would work hard to keep music and art alive in the schools. In this context my mother became active in the Massachusetts Art Council. There was a local group as well that would meet in Wilmington. Its focus was to keep the Arts alive in the community and to run programs to generate people's interest in the Arts.

In fact, my mother was instrumental in getting permission to obtain the current Arts Council Building as the group's official location (across from the Protestant Church). It was probably in the mid to late 1970s that the Art Council started to raise money for their fledgling Art group.

I remember hearing my mother run some ideas by my father at night when she would come home from these meetings. One night, my mother was explaining the idea that the local Arts group had decided on for fundraising.

The group, with my mother's help, designed a ticket, hand painted and quite pretty, about a 5 x 7 size, which people could purchase for five dollars each. The plan was that all the money would go into a local lottery. The idea also offered people to choose five numbers or so as part of the ticket. I don't remember how often the plan was for initially drawing the winner, whether it was every week or every month, but the idea was that the winner of the lottery would win all the money in the pool.

My mother was very excited about this idea, and she sketched some pretty designs for these tickets. I remember feeling badly for my mother, because at first my father scoffed at the idea, saying that no one was going to spend five dollars on this ticket. I remember my parents bantering back and forth, and I think there was some discussion that the Arts group was considering dropping the ticket amount down to one or two dollars. But the bottom line was that this idea went forward under the Massachusetts Arts Council group, and each local group, including the Wilmington chapter, was part of it.

Well, much to everyone's surprise, this idea really took off. Interestingly enough, my mother, who was never very good with money anyway, came home one night after one of the local Arts meetings. She told my father the Arts Council was making so much money from these tickets they had to elect a Treasurer for their local Wilmington group, and for some reason, the group elected my mother.

It's rather funny now, but my mother, who was so smart in Science, History, and English, had no head for numbers. She ended up bringing the money home after every meeting so my father actually had to help her and play the role of "behind the scenes" Treasurer. It got to be a bit of a joke in our household that my mother was actually involved in this big money-making idea.

At some point, as the government will do when any private group is making a significant amount of money, the State of Massachusetts stepped in and wanted to take over this lottery activity. I remember my parents discussed this as well, because the Arts Council group worked so hard to fight for its existence and they came up with this idea, and all of a sudden it was going to be taken over by the State.

There were a lot of meetings that followed with the State over this, and the Arts Council did work out with the State that a portion of the lottery money would still be used to fund the Arts in Massachusetts.

Well, as it turns out, the Arts Council's fundraising enterprise was indeed taken over by the State and evolved into the now popular Massachusetts Megabucks lottery system, and now a lottery game that most states have instituted in one way or another.

My mother, in her later years, was always a little disappointed because she felt that the State of Massachusetts never did use the portion of the profits from Megabucks to support the Arts as they had originally promised.

The above are my personal memories of what went on with my mother's efforts in our household. I did Google this little bit of history in Massachusetts, but I could only find scant information about it. There was one article that mentioned how in 1971 a local Arts advocate, Jacqueline O'Reilly, conceived the idea of using a lottery, and a portion of the profits were to be given to the arts.

In the end, Mrs. O'Reilly and other advocates (one of these advocates being my mother and the local Wilmington Arts Council) worked together to come up with a program that would support community arts in Massachusetts. In 1973, the State Legislature established a Special Committee on the Arts to investigate ways of improving state arts funding at the community level in response to federal funding cuts to arts and culture.

In 1976, the idea for a state lottery was introduced as a source of revenue for the Arts. In 1979, the legislation authorized the formation of the Massachusetts Arts Lottery Council (MALC), and cities and towns began organizing the local Culture Councils to distribute funds. On October 14, 1980, the first Arts Lottery tickets went on sale and the tickets were five dollars. The first jackpot was $200,000.

I am proud that my mother, a proud Wilmington parent and teacher, Antoinette Campbell, was a part of this little piece of history.

It's also interesting that the person who wrote the article I found through my research, also voiced a similar disappointment about how the State of Massachusetts had diverted the proceeds initially promised for the Arts to multiple other purposes, therefore disappointing those in the Arts Council, like my mother, who struggled so hard over the years to keep Arts alive in Wilmington and beyond.

Free Range Kids

Group Conversations

Tom Mirisola, a longtime friend and Wilmington resident, had recently mentioned that in the '50s and '60s we grew up carefree, independent, and perhaps even reckless. So, we were truly "free range kids." In our younger years we ran free. We explored our limited universe with unlimited enthusiasm. We discovered the wonders of our small world and learned to appreciate them.

Being a 'free range kid' was a badge on honor.

"I like that term, "free range kids", too! I came to Wilmington with my family in 1953. We lived down on Shawsheen Ave near Billerica on Route 129 down near the other side of Trow's Farm," **Sandra Enos Conwell** says. *"I was eleven and allowed to ride my bike over to my aunt's and cousin's house on Andover Street, which was on the other side of town. I just had to call my Mom when I got there to let her know I didn't get killed on the old Shawsheen Ave bridge crossover to Main Street. A good ride, a safe trip, and priceless freedom! The good old days."*

Joyce Eaton Dalton adds, *"There weren't any worries when I grew up in the thirties and forties. I would walk down town at ten years old to do errands for my mother."*

"When I was about five or six years old my mother would give me a quarter to go to Tattersall's to buy a pack of Pall Malls cigarettes for her," Wilmington resident **Martha Rose** comments.

"I loved being a "free range kid," **Sandy Longo Keeley** states. *"I often tell people what a fabulous childhood I had. I was almost nine years old when we moved from Woburn to North Wilmington in 1974. I'd get on my bike and ride it anywhere and everywhere with all my friends until we were either exhausted or it was dinner time. We often spent the last few minutes of daylight swimming in our pool. Good times, my friends. Good times."*

"During the summer of 1970 I was thirteen," **Diane Dizacomo** begins. *"Both my parents worked. My mother had set me up so I would be occupied. But I had other ideas.*

"I never went to the summer school I was supposed to attend. I also never went to the swimming lessons at the lake which Mom had paid ahead of time. So, instead, I spent every day that summer riding my pink Spider bike around

> town with my transistor radio hanging from the handlebars. I rode in the summer breeze with no hands (wheeee!) going to the lake. I'd stop to read the magazines at Weinberg's and DeMoulas, and get a tall Fanta at the gas station in the center of the depot.
>
> "I'd shop at Simon's and Grants, have a treat at Scottie's with my spare change I 'borrowed' from Dad's dresser. Generally, I just did the town on my own with no adult supervision.
>
> "That was my formal introduction to Wilmington. No one ever brought up the subject of summer school or swimming lessons. So neither did I! It was the best summer of my life."

"*I grew up as a third generation Wilmingtonite. It was a wonderful town to grow up in,*" **Mary Lou Govoni** says. *"Loved the neighborhood with all the kids outside together all day, winter or summer. It was like having a very large family, which I did have."*

Michelle Giroux Higgs agrees. *"Yes, those were carefree days. The town's recreational department was opened and the schools were staffed for summer activities. We would pack our lunches in the morning and hop on our bikes and* head to the Boutwell School for a day of kickball, dodge ball, field trips, and Arts & Crafts. Then we were on our own until Mom rang the Giroux cowbell to come in for supper at 5:15.

"After supper we were back outside with our neighbors—the Connollys, Amaros, and Duffys, playing Kick-the-Can or Dodge Ball or Old Lady Witch or Red Rover or Tag until it got dark. Perhaps that's why we all became independent adults."

"Where I lived was a stone's throw away from many awesome adventures," **Sammie Lunt** recalls. "There was Patches Pond and the 'woods and fields of glory! I grew up with six brothers and they were explorers and creators. Behind our home were underground forts and aboveground strongholds. There was a 'top' and a 'bottom' field to play in and run in and drive in. We ran dirt bikes and 4-wheelers and wheelbarrows, whatever had wheels!

"We found turtles nesting and bee hives and wild blueberries and blackberries galore! We went fishing and swimming and rafting and skating on that frozen pond back there. In the 'woods' was a gully and the hill we sled on for years. It was available to us. Only the neighbors and friends knew about it. It was the best secret ever!

"On that same hill to the right was a long rope hanging from a tree. We called it the

"Tarzan" swing. It was the best fun a kid could have. But, the swing was tied off between trees, so thinking back it may not have been the safest place. However, kids would be kids. I'll never forget the fun we had back there always having fun outside in those days."

> My grandkids wanted to know what it was like growing up when I was a kid, so I shut off their Internet, took their Smart phones away, and told them to go play outside until dark.

Michael DiGregorio remembers when *"the Moore Street gang would play ice hockey on the frozen cranberry bog well after dark until we couldn't find the puck."*

"I loved skating at the cranberry bog!" **Terry Gustus** adds. *"There were stumps all over it, so it trained us to be agile on our blades! As kids we*

also walked alone to "The Little Yellow Store" on Shawsheen Ave for penny candy when we were only five or six years old. We also walked alone in the first grade from Ferguson Road to the West School. Try that today."

Robin Marsh reminisces, *"I love the accurateness of the term "free range kid." My family moved to town from Everett when I was five. So, technically I'm not a townie, but pretty close at this point fifty years later.*

"I remember riding my bike EVERYWHERE! Hiking in the woods behind our house, either alone or with friends for hours. Playing with the kids in the neighborhood until the Fire Horns went off. My mother was hard of hearing and was always surprised that I could make it home by 9:05 on a summer night without a watch. Mom never heard the horns until after I got married and lived much closer to the fire station where they were much louder. We had a good laugh about that.

"I remember as a teenager riding my horse from my house over to Salem Street near Tewksbury to my friend's house off Forest Street close to Burlington. While in junior and high school I walked over half a mile just to catch the bus. All the moms in the neighborhood would let you know if you did something wrong. Growing up as a free range kid helped shape my independence and self-confidence. I'm so glad to

> *have grown up here in Wilmington. I would definitely NOT have been a free range kid in the city."*

"*Behind my house on Woburn Street before the housing developments on Allen and Elm Streets, we would snow mobile all the way to Stelio's and then go sledding. There was a horse race track back there as well, that we road around. We had so much fun as kids,"* **Leanne Bishop Woodland** remembers.

"*Wilmington was a wonderful place to up in the fifties,"* **Donald C. Hubbard** adds. "*We were outside from morning to dusk. Had to be home when the street lights came on. We had the woods and fields and the bog to explore. We rode our bikes everywhere. It's a very different place now."*

Sharon Kelley recalls, "*My brothers and I grew up on Oakdale and skated Lubbers Brook for miles back in the '60s. Didn't come home 'til it got dark!!"*

"*I can remember getting out of Glen Road School and running home to get my baseball glove or street hockey stick, and then head back to the school to play,"* **Andrew Leverone** says. "*All the kids from Glen Road and Cunningham Street,* *basically anyone in the area, would meet there and play until dinner."*

Brian McCue adds, *"I remember going 'uptown' when I was like seven or eight. Or going over to the plaza when I was a year or two older. This was in the early '70s. We unfortunately moved to Florida soon after."*

"Off of Nichols Street we could cross the road and have miles of woods or skate on the bog or snowmobile. Now it's multiple developments," **Erin Antinarelli** shares.

"In the '60s you could ride your bike without fear." **Dennis Blair** remembers. *"I used to ride from Lloyd Road to Parker Ave where my cousin lived."*

Kathy Whitney Timmons says, *"Our house was between Salem Street and Route 62. There were tons of trails where we rode our ponies and bikes and skated on the pond before the development went in. Fun times. Sad that it's all so changed."*

"I don't ever remember asking Mom if I could go outside. We just went, as long as we were home for supper or when the street lights came on we were fine. There was a gang of us that ran together—the Gagnes, Butlers, Noni, and Chippy Richardson. Sometimes we had a theme, like Batman and Robin or Cowboys and Indians. We often made forts out of sticks and piles of leaves or pine needles.

"One summer I rode my bike everywhere, from Woburn Street to Lucci's Market or to meet my friend Jane at the drug store for a bottle of Coke along with some Clove gum. Or I'd ride up Federal Street along Wildwood to the library. There I would spend hours at the microfiche reading old newspapers. Or maybe ride all the way over to Wakefield around Lake Quannapowitt.

"My friends and I would ice skate across the street, flatten pennies on the railroad tracks, pick blueberries for Saturday morning pancakes. We had our bikes and hula hoops and balls and jacks and huge jump ropes and lots of imagination. Sometimes we'd even go out and play in the puddles. 'Free range kids' describes us quite well." **Leslie Freeman**

"Back then it was pretty care free. You could ride your bike almost everywhere without fear. There *were lots of areas to move around without disturbing others. Lots of woods and fields to play in."* **Paul Bielecki** continues, *"The population had some seasonality to it, though greatly reduced from the 1920s through the very early '50s."*

Bob Murphy adds a somewhat scary but humorous story. *"I am missing a portion of the cartilage in my right ear. It was eaten by a horse! Specifically, it was eaten by a horse in Harnet's barn off Woburn Street. We kids were playing there when I got knocked down back to a stall door, startling the horse. He/she did what was natural and reached over the stall door and bit me! Nobody sued, but I still have hearing loss."*

"The '70s and '80s were 100% free range as well," adds **Bryan Webster**

Sandra Berrigan Fallica agrees, *"I think the '70s & '80s kids as latchkey kids. We definitely had free range too since then both parents started holding jobs."*

"I grew up on Chestnut Street. We had a golf course on one end of the street and an open air hockey rink with light at the other end," **Bob Wolley** recalls. *"We would play hockey from dawn all day and half the night in the winter. (It was a little illegal with the lights thing.)*

"Summer time was golf with my grandpa playing the 7th and 8th holes over and over (again, slightly frowned upon). This was in the '60s and '70s. What a blast. It was a great childhood."

"We also had the old Duffy farm land across the street from us where we spent hours playing and driving our ATC90 three-wheeler off road. In the winter we pulled kids on their skis and drove through the woods to the cranberry bogs on Shawsheen Ave," adds **Michele Giroux Higgs**.

"Then we'd ice skate for hours with our tape recorders making up routines. Many side streets off Aldrich Road had water, so we could skate for hours on end on bumpy ice along the narrow trails. They were the good old days!"

Michele Bee shares her memories as a free range kid. *"Being a kid in Wilmington, my Mom would wrap a hot plate for us to bring to my brother Bobby at the Jenny Station. (I can still hear the 'ding-ding' from the hose whenever a car drove over it.)*

"We would wait at the triangle at the end of Bridge Lane and Route 38. Bobby would walk across the two lane road to get his dinner and always gave us change for a soda.

"Mom would walk us down to that triangle patch of land every Veteran's Day and pay respect to the men of Wilmington who died in

> Vietnam. They were young men who grew up in the area.
>
> "There are so many memories of walking around town with friends. Walking on the jagged wall in front of Rocco's on the way up Main Street to Tattersall's. Walking to the carnival next to St. Dorothy's and at the Town Common. My sister would walk us to church, and I remember a few times stopping at Weinberg's to get candy on the way."

"I remember going to the Shawsheen River by the Aqueduct off Route 129 or down the tracks (usually without parental permission). We'd fish with just sticks and whatever we could find for bait. Then, for hours we would hunt and catch turtles. In the winter, skating at the old cranberry bog was a must! We had so much fun and would be there all day!" **Renee Pineau** says.

Tom Beaton recalls, "Our mother always told us to get out of the house and go play outside. I remember playing baseball and football at the Glen Road School with friends. We had no uniforms or referees, but it didn't much matter. We shot baskets in the winter standing on snow banks. We rode our bikes all over Wilmington without helmets."

"In the summer if we were not at the North Intermediate playground we would put our bathing suits on under our clothes and ride our bikes to the lake to swim. Sometimes we'd double up on our bikes so everyone could go," **Mary Winnett Giroux** remembers.

"We also picked buckets of wild blueberries, either at Harold Parker or at the bogs off the tracks. At home we would eat blueberry pancakes for weeks.

"In the winter we would skate on the wetlands off the railroad tracks. We had a fort there and would build a fire to stay warm while we played pond hockey all day. Back then, they would also flood the tennis courts behind the North Intermediate.

"As free range kids we would roam around all day. Build forts, play impromptu soccer games, and just have fun. There was no schedule, just hours to roam."

Betty Webb shares a few memories. *"My dad, Bill Nee, was a firefighter. We would walk down to the fire station and he would treat us kids to bottles of real Coke! We also used to get the fountain drinks at Woodside's Pharmacy.*

"I remember the whole neighborhood of kids walking together from Harris Street through the back roads to Silver Lake. In the winter we'd

skate on Patches Pond. Back then we grew up climbing trees, building forts, and playing outdoor games."

"I grew up on Harold. The Shawsheen commons didn't exist yet and we would all make forts and play in the woods," **Jacqueleen Fonseca** shares. "Once the commons was built, the neighborhood kids would all meet for football games. It didn't matter if you were a boy of a girl; we just had fun and tackled. We'd all go out in the morning after breakfast and meet up. Just had to be home by dinner time. Simpler times."

> "I fondly remember those days when kids felt safe and parents felt safe allowing their children out to play," **Susan Patterson** confirms. "We moved to Wilmington when it was still country, from Somerville in 1964 when I was three years old."

"I used to leave my house in the morning, go to a friend's house, and then head out on our bikes or roam through the woods. Someone's mother always had lunch for us kids, I just had to call home and say where I was. Then we'd be back out to play. The only rule was to be home when the street lights came on," **Laurie Carrasco Lowman** shares her experience as a kid.

"The best memories were the recreation clubs at the schools during the summer. There were so many activities, field trips, and great youth counselors. That's where I met Mike Esposito. He was one of the counselors and took me under his wing.

"I also remember we always looked for the house where all the bikes were because that was where you knew all your friends were. Wilmington was a great place to grow up as 'free range.'

"I used to love going to the St. Dorothy's Holiday Bizarre each year. I attended Mildred Rogers School and have stayed by the lake to this day. I ended up buying the property next to the one I grew up in," **Dorene Messieri** remembers.

"I tell my granddaughter stories of what it was like growing up back then and she finds penny candy the most difficult to believe.

"I am proud to live in Wilmington and proud to have made so many awesome friends over the years. I feel honored to be called a 'townie.' Many fond memories of days gone by."

Laura Blair confirms, "I loved growing up in Wilmington! Lots of memories, whether they were happy or sad, they're memories I will treasure."

Wilmington's 'Little Rascals' Gang

Photo Courtesy of Tony Meads

August 1963

L. to R. : Billy Gray, Robin Meads, Tom Mirisola, Steven Johnson, Bob Johnson, Martha Meads, Anthony Meads (Face Covered) Ricky Gray

Center: Phillip Lippens (Robin Meads visiting cousin)

And... Pal the Dog

The picture was taken by Robin Meads Mother in their front yard. Across the street in the background is Mattucci's House and front yard. It always had a large weeping willow tree and the big boat that never left the yard.

We're sitting or leaning on one of our homemade go carts we constructed using whatever materials we had available. We raced cart(s) on the Dewey Ave. Hill alongside your house.

Not in the picture: Eddie Johnson and Ralphie Van Steensburg who were off making their own cart to race against ours.

In Honor of John J. Fullerton
Fallen Heros: Part II
by Fred Shine

John J. Fullerton, Jr., U.S. Army, 52nd Inf., Company B, Military Police. He was killed on January 29th, 1968, during the Tet Offensive at the Saigon Embassy in Vietnam.

Jackie and other MPs held off the attack on the U.S. Embassy. Nine MPs were riding in a half track when it was struck by an anti-tank rocket, disabling the vehicle. They then came under heavy fire from the surrounding buildings. All nine men were killed.

Jackie was a typical Lake Kid, like me. We played together, fought together, pushed each other into Silver Lake, and had been friends since childhood. Jackie's Mom and Dad worked at WHS. His Dad was a custodian and his Mom worked in the cafeteria. Jackie played football for WHS and was a full back, # 32! He came from a large family and lived on Main St. near the Tewksbury line.

In March of 1982 the country finally paid tribute to the Veterans of the Vietnam War and began the construction of the Vietnam Veteran's 'Black Wall' in Washington D.C.

In searching for a proper memorial site for Jackie, I was given the option and permission from the town for a parcel of land on Main Street bordering Silver Lake, right near Jackie's home. It was across from the old Wilmington TV Repair shop on the beach that we called The Drop.

It was a perfect location except for a small detail. Jackie's sister had a baby son, named John, after his deceased uncle. Her son was hit and killed by a car at that very spot while exiting a school bus. Needless to say, it was not a good site for his monument. Jackie's Mom told me that location brought back too much pain and bad memories whenever she passed it. So, of course that site was out of the question.

However, further up Grove Ave, across from where Paul McMelville lived, was a large parcel of land that once had an old store, some apartment buildings which had been torn down years before, and had become an eye sore with its old trash barrels, tree stumps, and trash and overgrown weeds.

The land was situated beside Town Beach, and the parcel itself was known to us as Fuller's Beach. It was a perfect spot, but needed a lot of work. With the help of Mr. Downs and the highway department, construction of the Fullerton Park began.

In the planning of the site, Rocco DePesquale, had a great idea for that spot too, and we worked together to make it happen. He thought it would be an ideal location to add a parking lot and a

Handicapped Access Fishing Pier. Sad to say years later, after Rocco had passed away, the pier was built, but 'other people' took credit for it and never mentioned Rocco's name.

The stone monument was to be another piece of granite from the Jenks Bridge. It was a peaceful and large park coming along beautifully with no problems. Well, almost none. The neighbors were thrilled that I finally got the eye sore cleaned up. The dedication was being planned and Mr. Downs approached me with an idea. He told me the Vietnam Veterans Wall in DC had some extra black granite.

We contacted them and were able to get four slabs, each 12" long by 4" tall. We had the stone master who had engraved the DC memorial etch the names of the four Wilmington boys exactly as they appeared on the original monument. Then on Mother's Day I presented the mothers of all four boys with the granite (except Jackie's Mom) and it stood as "my commitment" to build a monument for them.

Then as the individual monuments were built I would come to take that granite and have it embedded in the stone so people who could never go to DC could get a 'Rubbing.' Wilmington was documented as being the first and only town to have an actual piece of a National Monument as part of its local memorial. It was big news and appeared in Boston newspapers. Jackie's was the First!

We (the DAV and family) planned to meet across the street where the old DAV had burnt down, and march across Grove Ave to the site. However, the news of the granite brought some big surprises. I was getting calls from bands and politicians and various groups asking to be part of my "Parade to honor Vietnam Veterans."

I hadn't planned on a parade, but it was happening. We ended up gathered at the old Glen Road School, and the parade, with high school bands, and drum corps and other groups kept growing. We marched down Glen Road to Main St, up Grove Ave to the site. People stood on the side watching the entire procession. When we arrived, groups were still leaving Glen Road. Jackie's parents and family were very proud of the turn out for their son.

Now the ceremony didn't go off quite as planned. It rained for three days prior and the park was soggy. It was still drizzling on the morning of the parade and I had former state representatives and senators approaching me, and asking to speak. I grabbed some index cards, put their names on them, and put them in my pocket. The day before I had gone to the site and in my mind pictured where everyone would stand and where the podium would be placed. I looked at Jackie's monument and thought, "Something was missing."

It needed something else! I knew what it was missing. Flowering Azalea bushes, red! Jackie loved them. So I called my landscaper friend and that night he placed the flowers, one on each side of the stone, beside the evergreen bushes.

At the site, and with all the rain, the loud speaker system had gotten wet and shorted out. (Damn it)! I called my friend Toddy from Arlington Fire and Rescue and told him my dilemma. No problem! He grabbed a civil defense truck and, lights flashing, raced to Wilmington. Boy, was I happy the parade turned out to be so long! Toddy arrived in plenty of time to set up and we had sound!

Channel 4 WBZ TV showed up to film the entire event. It was a BIG occasion for our town. The Wilmington Minutemen brought their cannons and fired volleys across the lake at given times during the ceremony. Boy, were they loud! NOW THE FUN begins!

I opened the dedication ceremony and took those index cards out to pick out my guest speakers. Well, silly me. All the cards were wet and the ink ran. I couldn't read a single one. I held them up to the crowd and said, "Well, I can't read these, so if you want to speak, find me between speakers and give me your name again."

Mrs. Fullerton looked upset. All my work was being disrupted. Again, no problem! I called the first speaker I knew, U.S. Senator Bob Bull, who was always there for me. I stepped back to allow him to approach AND....I fell over that darn

Azalea bush, fell backwards and slid down toward the lake in some mud.

The TV cameraman quickly took the camera off me. I got up, mud on my pants, and saw the tears coming to Mrs. Fullerton's eyes! I looked up at the sky and yelled, "Damn it Jackie! WHY did you choose today to push me in the lake AGAIN!" Jackie's Mom started to laugh and said, "You two boys were always pushing one another in the lake! HE'S HERE! JACKIE IS HERE!"

The rest of the ceremony went on without a problem. I do believe Jackie was there!

Jackie's family always visits the monument on Memorial Day, and one of his family members who has "earned the privilege," usually one of the grandchildren, gets to walk up with me and place a wreath. Mrs. Fullerton was able to finish her life knowing her son was honored. When Mr. Fullerton died, their family asked me to be a pallbearer since he had considered me to be one of his sons. It was quite an honor!

Jackie Fullerton's Monument is a beautiful park with a playground at the town beach (dedicated to Sean Collier, the Policemen killed by the Boston Marathon Bombers) and the Handicapped Fishing Pier. Jackie's grand nephews are always there fishing.

The Day Family and Wilmington

By Carol Day Boisvert

I didn't grow up in Wilmington. My earliest memories, before I moved here in 1980, were the annual Memorial Day visits to the Wildwood Cemetery.

Dad, Mom, and I would load the car with flowers. Geraniums, marigolds, and petunias were packed inside as we headed toward the cemetery. I realize now that my two brothers, Stanley Jr.'s and Steve's presence wasn't necessary, as it would not be their responsibility to continue our yearly tradition. That would be mine.

We'd pull into the cemetery, drive around the stone caretaker's building, and park right across from the baptismal pool, which in the 1950s and 1960s was full of frogs and lily pads.

This is where my Wilmington story begins.

Yes, my brother Steve moved to town first. Then my family moved here as well, so we do have recent roots here too. But, it's the historical piece of my story I want to share, and it is a most interesting account.

As a child, the names and dates etched into the many cemetery headstones were meaningful to me and represented my personal history. They had a direct impact on me. However, it was my brother Steve who dove into the historical and genealogical past that I write about here.

Steve did so in hopes that the Wilmington Historical Society would change the plaque name located at 190 Middlesex Ave from the Blaisdell House to the Captain Stephen Palmer Day House. Here was his reasoning based on his research.

According to records, Stephen Day had purchased the house on April 29, 1826 from Henry Carter, and it remained in the Day family for forty-five years until 1871. Stephen had married Sarah Frost in 1805. He served as a

sergeant in the militia in the war of 1812 and was later promoted to captain. Both he and Sarah are buried in the Wildwood Cemetery.

The Middlesex home was later willed to Stephen's three sons: Stephen, Thomas, and John. Wife Sarah and her son Stephen lived in the house for the remainder of her life. Four years after Sarah's passing in 1867, Stephen sold the property to the widow Lavinia Blaisdell who lived there until 1890.

Thomas was my great-grandfather and is also buried in Wildwood, along with his first wife Rosannah (who had passed at thirty years of age from tuberculosis) and his second wife, my great-grandmother, Clara Melissa Smith Day.

My grandparents, Albert Cornelius Day and Margretta Adelaide Day, and my parents, Stanley Warren Day and Anna Arvida Swanson Day, are also in the same resting place with many of my other relatives. I could genuinely say that my family roots are in this town.

My brother Stephen Lawrence Day and his family moved to Wilmington in 1972, so our legacy continues.

Remember when...
...sleeping out on the front porch was an adventure

The Blizzard of '78
Survivors' Memories

New England winters can be brutal and sometimes they are 'wicked bad.' The massive blizzard back in February 1978 was one of the worst snow storms we lived through. More than two feet of snow had fallen in a little more than a day. Roads were impassable, people were stranded, many lost electrical power and heat, and people died. The entire town, along with much of the Northeast, was shut down and many were left on their own to survive. Here are some memories of that time.

"When my mom and I lost power we lived on Main Street," **Jane Woods** begins. *"We took what we needed and decided to walk to my grandmother's house on Cottage St. We left our driveway by leaping over a huge snow bank. We walked in the street for about one minute and realized that a large truck was coming toward us.*

"All of a sudden a man appeared and helped pull us over the snow bank out of the path of the oncoming truck. The visibility was terrible, and I'm sure the truck driver would not have seen us. Thank goodness our neighbor was outside and saw us. I will never forget that."

Susan Taylor Given Wass clearly remembers the storm. *"I lived on Middlesex Ave in Wilmington at the time. I worked at a nursing home in Woburn and had to go in for my shift. I had to hang my head outside my car's side window to see where I was going because the snow was coming down so fast my wipers couldn't keep the windshield clear.*

"I was lucky enough when I came to the Woburn line a police officer stopped me. He asked where I was going, and of course I told him. He gave me a police escort to my job. He was a great guy."

"At that time we had a beautiful wood burning stove. Perfect for that day," recalls **Shirley Pumfrey**

Even as a youngster back then, **Jacqui Pappalardo** still has memories of the storm. *"I was only four years old but I do remember my mom pulling us kids on a sled heading to Lucci's! I also remember hearing about the 'Blizzard of '78' for my entire life during every snowstorm thereafter."*

"We lived on Jacquith Road and lost power for a while," **Elaine DePasquale** says. *"The stock of firewood kept us warm. No one could drive for days except for emergency vehicles. Like a lot of

people, we walked to the convenience store for food. Sal made a lot of money plowing snow."

"I remember having no power, but we had a kerosene stove that heated the basement. All of our doors were blocked by drifts of snow eight feet high," **Leeann Sadowski** shares. *"I remember my dad had to remove the glass from a storm door to dig a path to the oil tank to get more kerosene. We have a picture somewhere of him climbing through the storm door."*

George Keith relays his story as a kid after the storm. *"Being twelve years old, my friends and I dug tunnels through the snow banks and made forts and igloos out of snow. It was the best winter a kid could ever have. I remember climbing to the top of the fire escape behind Church Street Hardware and jumping down into the fresh snow. It had to be fifteen feet in the air. With shovels we cleared the pond of snow so we could play ice hockey and it was like boards in a rink. We made a fortune shoveling. Nobody does that anymore. Hahaha!"*

"We lived on Brand Ave, but when the Route 129 bridge was built our road became a dead end. Neighbors and family friends (all the Marden boys helped my Dad) came out of the woodwork to help everyone shovel out to get to the doors of

the houses! The town plow trucks piled the snow so high up at the church at the other end of our road," **Michele Bee** recalls.

"My brothers and I made forts as tall as DeMoulas! We also built some of the best snow castles. We didn't have school forever. Friendly's was open, and after playing in the snow all us neighborhood kids would get an ice cream cone! They were some of the best memories of being a kid! Being outside, skating everywhere, and sledding down the broken Bridge Lane bridge!!"

"We had to go stay at my grandmother's house because she had a fireplace to keep warm," **Kim Cullivan Baron** adds.

Thomas Jillett remembers, "I was driving around town during that storm, going nuts spinning out of control on purpose. That's how I learned to drive in the snow."

Tom Beaton shares his story. "I shoveled for thirteen hours. As always, the Wilmington highway department did a fantastic job plowing. I was driving around town the next day on nicely plowed roads while the rest of Massachusetts under the Governor's orders was told to stay home because driving was too dangerous."

"I had to jump out my second story bedroom window to start shoveling after the storm. My Mum was a nurse at Choate and had to get a ride from the Wilmington police to go to her shift," **Lori A. Ingersoll Carlo** adds.

"My dad plowed for the state at the time so he was gone for a few days. When he came home, a pine tree had fallen through our living room," **Whitney Timmons** vividly remembers. *"Our ponies were stuck in our barn/garage. My brother and sister and I had to shovel (what seemed like hours) just to get them out. We all survived, amazingly without cell phones or the Internet."*

Lisa Stira adds, *"I remember shoveling and shoveling! We could hear the trees snapping in the woods that surrounded our house on Boutwell. The skiing that year was amazing."*

141

"I also remember the blizzard of '78! The snow at the end of the driveway was so tall the kids rode down them on their sleds. There was no work since the state was shut down. No trains running and cars were ordered to stay off the roads. Most of us had no power for several days.

"All us gals with children would gather to form a parade of sleds. We'd hike up to Lenny & Maria's store on Route 38, right over the Wilmington line," **Sandra Enos Conwell** recalls. *"They had no power also, but opened with kerosene lamps for necessities. Oh. They sold beer, wine, and liquor too. The kids would get candy and cookies. The adults...well, the adults got their stuff!*

"We slept in sleeping bags in the living room near the fireplace and had all the peanut butter and jelly sandwiches anyone could eat! Umm...and the goodies from Lenny & Maria's. Funny though, we all look back on those days with happy memories."

Deborah Shine Harrington says, *"Work sent everyone home before the storm got really bad. Had to dig down to find my car, which was also snow white. The snow bank was high enough that one of our dogs sat on the roof, kind of like Snoopy."*

> *"We shoveled for days and days, it seemed. The snow banks were so high you couldn't see over them. We built snow tunnels and forts in front of our house and had snowball wars. We also walked down to the North Intermediate School. The snow drifts were so tall we would climb onto the ledge around the gym and jump into them. We used lots of bread bag liners for our boots,"* **Mary Winnett Giroux** remembers.
>
> *"Back then we wore the ski mobile parkas with the fake fur around the hood. Everyone had one. You could walk anywhere in the middle of the street since there were no cars. If we lost power we had a wood burning stove to keep warm, and my Dad was a whiz with the Coleman camper stove. My Mom was a labor and delivery nurse, and needed a ride to work because the roads were so horrible."*

"I remember all the camaraderie when we finally were able to dig out of our homes!" adds **Jane Swisher Cannizaro**

Willis Whalen will always remember, *"I had just bought a 1978 Triumph Spitfire and dropped it off at the dealer for its 2000 mile check-up just as the snow started. Didn't see it again for ten days!"*

Terry Gustus recalls, *"There were two parts to that storm. Bill and I were leaving for the Peace Corps in Malaysia. We were on the plane and the blizzard had started up again. Our runway got plowed across. We were on the plane many, many hours before takeoff. Everyone was partaking of the free drinks and movies. Finally took off and got to Malaysia. The headline in the English language newspaper read, 'Boston Blizzard'."*

"I remember being thankful I had gas when we lost electricity," **Shirley Pumfrey** says. *"All the neighbors were over heating water for coffee, tea, and washing."*

Donna Richards Aronofsky remembers, *"I was nineteen and working at a retirement home in Chestnut Hill. I made it to work that morning, but then couldn't leave for a few days. Not many employees made it in so I worked MANY hours. When I could finally leave, I drove up Route 128 with HUGE piles of snow on both sides of the highway. No one else was on the road. It was like driving through a tunnel."*

"We were running low on food because there was no driving allowed. My best friend Robin and I, both seventeen, walked to Billerica to a little convenience store. I bought frozen fish sticks for dinner. We realized after cooking them, they were spoiled!" **Becky Lightizer** recalls. *"I wrote to*

the company to complain about my hike in the blizzard to get food. They sent me coupons for more fish sticks!"

Janice McInnis Babineau sadly remembers, *"My twelve year old nephew died in the blizzard. He and his friend sat in a car while it was warming up. The tailpipe was clogged with snow and they both died."*

"I was working on Summer Street in Boston at BCBS and was able to get home in four hours!" **Christine Emery Goodwin** says. *"I packed my skis and left for New Hampshire to stay with friends. Got paid for nine days while Boston was closed and skied the entire time, including disco dancing in Manchester at night!"*

"I remember having to climb out the second story window to get out of the house because the snow was higher than the door," **Lee A. Jewels** adds. *"We were climbing onto the roof from the nearest window. Being a kid then was awesome, especially when we had a couple weeks of school off."*

Leanne Cummings shares a memory from that time. *"I was nineteen and living on Kelley Road in Wilmington while working as a secretary at Polyvinyl Chemical Industry. I couldn't believe I* *was actually getting paid to stay home since we were in a State of Emergency.*

"I remember we couldn't get out the doors or garage because the snow was so deep. I was able to climb out our kitchen window and shovel the front steps so we could get outside! I'll never forget the Blizzard of '78!"

"I survived shoveling the driveway. I think the snow was as tall as I was and the driveway was long," adds **Clare O'Beirne Brady**

Paul Keough says, *"I was a senior in high school working at Sweetheart Plastics. All I could see of my '67 Camaro was the antenna when my shift ended. I walked to the police station where Officer Cuoco gave me a ride home."*

Robert Eagan remembers, *"I grew up on Andover Street and I remember the Carlson family. Dick had a couple of snowmobiles. One of his daughters went out to rescue people."*

Terri O'Conners Allum *"I was at my home on Williams Ave with my three children, David Jr., three and a half years old, Kelli, two and a half, Johannah, one and a half, and I was seven months pregnant. My husband was on a business trip in Chicago. Our furnace oil lines froze up, so we had no heat except for the fireplace. The house dropped down to 38 degrees.*

"My Dad, Tom O'Conners, drove over and we packed up the kids. I followed him to my Nana's on Swain Road where we dropped off my baby daughters. My son and I followed Dad down Burlington Ave to Chestnut Street in the middle of the blizzard. You couldn't tell what side of the road you were on. I was driving a Ford Pinto station wagon which wasn't the best vehicle to be on the road during a storm.

"We stayed at my parents' home on Chestnut for a week. My husband was calling from Chicago saying he would be home in a day. I explained there was no way he was gong to make it home. All the airports were closed and there was a ban on travel.

"He eventually made it home on Saturday after the storm and couldn't believe the amount of snow. We finally went home and the fuel pipes had thawed. Luckily no pipes had burst. Two months later, our fourth child, Tom, was born."

Lu-Ann Pozzi remembers, "We lived on Allen Park Drive and I remember the roads were so icy we could skate down them. We also delivered groceries to my elderly grandmother using a sled."

"We had just moved in November. I woke up to go to work and couldn't get out of the house because the snow blocked both doors," **Joan Arsenault Phillips** recalls. "I had to go through *the basement door after my husband shoveled out a path."*

"We lived in an apartment in Dracut at the time. My Gremlin barely made it up the hill. We had four cases of beer and six bottles of vodka and played a lot of poker that week," **Jack Virtus** admits. *"Paid for the booze!"*

Lisa Bernard Coolbaugh adds, *"We walked on the empty, snow-covered roads. And of course, no school for a week!"*

"I was 19 and working with my mother at a medical device facility. We rode home in a carpool that day to the best of my recollection, and it took at least, if not more than two hours to get home. I enjoyed the two weeks of not being able to go anywhere and spending a pleasant time with my parents. I also stopped smoking, as easy access to cigarettes was not readily available," **Lisa Kennedy Cox** says.

Maureen Deveau Bedrosian relates her storm experience. *"My siblings were still living at home. I went out with my dad in his truck all through Wilmington and Tewksbury to help people who needed shoveling out, cutting and moving downed trees. Whatever had to be done, we did it. I don't know if dad knew the people or* *if he just drove around seeing who needed assistance."*

"I was twenty years old on that day. It surely was a crazy time," **Patricia Sullivan** recalls. *"I worked for McKesson and Robbins, and since it was a drug and medical supply company, we had to work. The National Guard would pick me up at my home and drive me back and forth to work. It was extremely hectic, but rewarding."*

Dianna Paulsen DiGregorio tells her story about surviving the blizzard. *"Forty-three years ago my husband and I got married on Saturday, February fourth, 1978.*

"It had snowed the day before and we were worried how people could get to the wedding due to the predictions of heavy snow. The wedding was at 11:00 AM and we slid into a snow bank. Luckily I made it to the church in time.

"The next day (Sunday) we drove to Vermont and stayed at a ski chalet which had a very long driveway. It had snowed through the night, and on Monday morning we couldn't see my car, which was a Firebird. It was buried, all except for the tip of the antenna.

"We had a man who came to plow us out, but there was too much snow for his truck to handle. He had to walk all the way to the chalet to tell us he would be back with a 'dozer.' (This was before cell phones.) We waited until Wednesday to get

plowed out as the dozers were clearing all the roads in the area. Once the roads were opened, we were able to get in some great skiing.

"At the end of the week it was time to go home, however, the state was shutdown and so no one was allowed to drive. We weren't sure we would be able to drive in Massachusetts, but we got home without incident. And now we have a great wedding story to tell."

Blizzard Problems
Told by Fred Shine

It was late 1977 after the 'Gas Crush.' The crisis eased gasoline to almost $.85 a gallon and car sales dropped. That's when I lost my job as a car salesman and ended up working for the Commonwealth of Massachusetts DPW.

I worked out of the 'Burlington Pit', off Cambridge St, and we were in charge of sections of Routes 128, 3, 3A, and 38. I started in a road crew picking up trash and cleaning out storm drains, but by that time I began to turn my life around and was taking night classes at Middlesex Community College.

One day my supervisor saw me studying at lunch time and asked me what was I reading. I told him an Accounting Course. He told me to come with him into the office and said, "You work in here now!" They needed help dispatching plows and keeping records of the independent crews hired for plowing, and also the records for gasoline used in the DPW trucks.

On the night the Blizzard of 78 started I had one of the DPW trucks that plowed route 3A, from Winchester to the Lowell Line pick me up on its way back to the pit so I wouldn't have to drive. I waited till I saw him go past my house toward the Lowell line, and then walked up to 3A and waited for his return trip for my ride.

At the top of my street there was a car with its hood up, not running, and a man standing there looking under the hood. The storm was at its peak and the wind was blowing the snow so hard you couldn't see in front of you. The man's car had been driving head into the storm, and the snow was blown inside his engine compartment which stalled it.

I told him the plows were coming soon and we had to get it running and out of the way. While I was looking inside the hood the man said he worked the third shift at Atlantic Gelatin in Stoneham and was heading to work. He lived in Billerica and I believe he said his last name was Gilchrest.

I suddenly noticed he wasn't doing anything, but just looking dazed and confused. Then he just threw his hands in the air, his head folded back, and down he went. Just as he fell the Burlington

Police happened to be driving by, noticed him on the ground, and stopped.

The guy was not breathing and the police attempted CPR. An ambulance came and took him to Laney Clinic. I called the police the next day to see how he made out. They said he suffered a major heart attack and never regained. They said he was most likely dead before he ever hit the ground.

That was the beginning of a two week, 24/7 working shift dispatching plows to open Route 128 and all the other major roads. I was the only dispatcher at the pit, so I slept there. The police and fire personnel would bring us food. It was a very interesting, and at times filled with funny shenanigans and weird situations. I worked there until the spring, when I took a job at Raytheon.

Butters Farm

By Christine E. Goodwin

Note: The historic Wilmington building was built in 1682 by William Butter, one of the earliest town settlers.

My parents purchased Butters Farm in 1963 from the elderly Snow sisters for $10,500. I was five years old when my family landed in Wilmington and I graduated in the WHS class of 1975.

After living there for so many years I remember Butters Farm's simplicity, its handsome chestnut beams, its extremely low, wide pine ceilings, and slanted floors. There were two English Bristol brick beehive ovens at the center of the house. And it had four unusable fireplaces. Dad was afraid the place would burn down if we ever lit a fire.

The interior doors had handmade latches. The walls were made of plastered horsehair and the windows were single pane. Butters Farm had no foundation under the house. When the wind would blow, it was cold. Beneath it was only a root cellar with a secret escape tunnel from days gone by.

When Dad and Mom bought the old property it came without running water. There was just a hand pump attached to a stone sink. There also was no modern heat source, only a coal-fueled potbelly stove. It had one bathroom with a five foot claw-foot tub (which later became a feeding tub for the horses) and no shower.

My parents were certified horse addicts while they both worked full time at outside jobs. The three of us initially ran a horse farm on the property from the three-hundred year old barn. In the early '70s we added a ten stall barn and years later expanded it even more.

Butters Farm was nationally known for breeding, training, and showing National Champion Appaloosa horses. Early on, my Mom, Velma, competed not only in the show ring, but did competitive trail riding, such as in the Vermont 3 Day, 100 Mile challenge.

My Dad, Paul, was into rodeo. For decades before the turn of the 21st century, both he and Mom bred, bought and sold hundreds of great show horses at Butters Farm. Their efforts helped to make the Northeast the most prolific Appaloosa region and second largest horse breed in the country.

The Emerys were founding members of several New England Appaloosa horse organizations. Many weekends, when not off showing, were spent with friends and customers coming and going, sometimes even camping out for the weekend parties held at Butters Farm. I remember one time finding someone sleeping under the clothes line on a Sunday morning after a bash.

As I became old enough I rode horses professionally, eventually winning fourteen National and World Championships. I was the youngest National Horse Show judge at eighteen. I coached amateur riders while training horses and managing the horse business with my family. I placed in my first National Show at the age of eight. At thirteen I was followed for six months by a photographer for National Geographic doing an article on girls and horses.

I knew the trials through Wilmington, Woburn, and Burlington well, along with my horsey neighbors down Chestnut Street. We rode the gas line, the high tension line, the old Mill Pond, the Mill, and over through the waste site in Woburn where the horses would always get spooked and shy away. They knew more than humans about what we'd all eventually learn.

We would often gather at Merrill Farm's horse show ring with the Galantes, the Rooneys, the Sanborns, the McDonalds, the Lunds, the Maroneys, and others.

I trained many of my mounts by riding the dirt road of our farm and on the hills of the Garden of Eden's abandoned golf course. They were the same hills I also learned to ski on. Later I skied with the gang from Ski Haus.

At the Garden of Eden, owner Mr. Pipes in the winter would make a rope tow from his rear jeep wheel so us locals could ski and sled. Caught many a bullfrog in his ponds too!

In 1984 I graduated from MMC with a degree in Diagnostic Ultrasound. A year later I blended my horse and medical interests with the Vet for the U.S. Equestrian Team. I co-founded one of the first mobile veterinary diagnostic ultrasound services in the country. Most of the preliminary research was done in our barn at Butters Farm. I believe my success was from my years of breeding horses with my parents.

In the town of Wilmington back in those days we knew our neighbors and supported our police. We skated at the outdoor rink at the old South School almost nightly in the winter. We rode our bikes in the summer across the back roads of the town to Silver Lake to swim.

Occasionally in high school on a hot summer night, well after midnight, I'd rendezvous with girlfriends and we'd bike ride all over town, free as a bird! It was a great childhood growing up in Wilmington with 'free range parents.' I thrived there. It was safe. I still have everlasting love and affection for Wilmington.

'Double or Nothing' ridden by Christine 1977

Games We Played
Active Youths

Sports was an active part of most every kid's life not long ago. We played in the fields and on the ice. We played in the woods and on the streets. We played in our backyards and the neighborhoods. We also played in organized sports in school and town leagues. It was a good thing. Here are shared examples of how we competed and exercised and learned about life.

•Loved being a lifeguard at Town Beach•Ice skated on the Shawsheen cranberry bog every winter afternoon•Playing pickup baseball games in Thompson Grove

•Yelling "Car!" when one was coming down the road•Skinny dipping in Silver Lake•The sting of those red dodge balls when you got hit in the face

•Learning to use a sail board on the lake•The day Mr. Kelley's track team beat Andover! •Pushing off the starter blocks in the 100 yard dash

•The sound of a bat hitting a home run in Little League•Pop Warner flag football •Bicycle races through the woods

•Skating on the swamp behind our house on Fairfield Road•Sledding on 'Suicide Hill' at the town park•Swinging on tall sapling trees like a monkey

- Summer camp at Boutwell School
- Swimming across Silver Lake●Playing ice hockey in the pits

- Ice skating behind the fire station●Riding your bike everywhere in town●Cheer leading the Wildcats on to victory

- Playing basketball on a donkey●Sunndaayy! New England Dragway! Route 101, Epping, NH!●Holding on for dear life to a rope tied around a tall branch as your friends pull

- Passing swimming classes by jumping out of a canoe at the lake and making it to Town Beach●Street hockey●Practicing softball under the high school tennis lights

- Watching the Thanksgiving Wilmington-Tewksbury football game from the cold bleacher seats●Climbing the ten foot tall jungle bars●North Intermediate vs. West Intermediate

- Memorial Day weekend clash of the classes' softball tournament●4-H horse shows in the mid-1950s●Walking the Wilmington ice rink with soda cans on our feet

- Football rally before the big game
- Spending a summer afternoon at Fenway Park
- Horseback riding ten miles each way from Woburn to Clark Farms

- Girl's field hockey behind the High School
- Playing badminton in the backyard
- Fishing for catfish in the bogs

- Jumping off a bridge into a water hole
- Cruising the lake on a fat inner tube
- Running the long cross country track around the High School

- Taking extra laps in the gym for mouthing off to the coach
- Hiking the woods to spy on other neighborhoods
- Climbimg a hill to be 'King of the Mountain'

- Red Rover, Red Rover, send Johnny right over
- Hop scotch
- Playing a game of horseshoes in the backyard

- Chasing the soccer ball for an hour
- Hitting the basketball courts under the night lights
- Watching the girls in their short uniforms playing tennis

Mr. Spanks, a Fire Escape, & Me

Written by Linda A. Arsenault
WHS Class of 1968

My mother could tell that I was not happy on the short walk to the school bus stop at the end of Dell Drive. The date was September 5, 1956 and it was my first day of school.

As we waited for the bus, we were joined by a few other children who, like me, were assigned to the Walker School for 1st and 2nd grades. As the bus came into view and the kids chose someone to sit next to, I stood back with my mother because I would be sitting on a reserved seat beside the bus driver.

That arrangement was one of the few concessions agreed between my parents and the school district in order for me to attend the same school with the other neighborhood children.

You see, I was born with Spastic Hemiplegia Cerebral Palsy. Cerebral Palsy is a birth injury caused by the lack of oxygen. In my case it affected my right side, resulting in my right leg being an inch shorter and weaker than my left leg. My right arm was also noticeably weaker than my left arm.

To help my mobility I wore a leather and elastic brace made specially for me by my physical therapist. That device was designed to keep me from dragging my leg.

For as long as I can remember, my parents Fred and Jean Arsenault raised me as their daughter first, and a child with a disability second. I was encouraged to try and do everything that my brothers, twelve year old Rick and four year old Glenn, were able to do. Those tasks usually took a lot of patience and perseverance, and luckily for me, my Scottish stubbornness.

I loved first grade. My teacher was Miss O'Brian, and she was wonderful. The first grade classrooms were on the first floor, so for me it was an easy walk up the stairs into the building with a left turn into Room 1.

The only other stairs to navigate during the day were the steps down to the lunchroom which was located in the basement. Also, once a week we had a class parade through the building to show off our best school papers.

I was allowed to take the time I needed to use the stairs during the day so I wouldn't hinder anyone else behind me. But I could usually keep up with everyone.

Second grade found me again in the Walker School, but that year I'd be in Mrs. Dunnigan's class on the second floor in Room 3. While I was happy to be with my neighborhood friends and first grade classmates, there was now a challenging second flight of stairs to go up and down multiple times a day.

I had always been able to climb stairs, but I sometimes grew tired, and that would slow me down. As the new school year began there were new things to get used to, including a Fire Drill from the second floor.

I assumed that we were to be directed to get in line and walk in single file down the central staircase and out the front door to the circular driveway, as we had done in first grade. But to my surprise we were led toward the far side of the classroom where a back door was open to a fire escape.

One by one we were to walk down the steep stairs and get in line on the school playground. I remember stepping on the fire escape grate landing, scared to death because I didn't have a comfortable feeling beneath my right foot, partially due to the grate's design and partially due to the lack of full feeling in my right leg.

I slowly and gingerly made it down those stairs, but it was not something I wanted to repeat anytime soon. As I was joining my class already standing in line, I noticed the school principle, Mrs. Keville, talking with the other teachers and our custodian Mr. Spanks.

It was apparent to everyone that in the event of an emergency my insecurity on the fire escape could potentially be a danger to the school's staff and students, and to myself attempting to get down the stairs on my own.

At that moment I was scared and mad at the same time. I was scared since I had trouble on the fire escape I wouldn't be able to stay at the Walker School. I was mad at myself because I didn't have two strong legs like everyone else, and I couldn't go down the stairs just like everyone else.

But, a possible solution was being discussed by Mrs. Keville and my teacher. I would learn about it from my parents a few days later. The plan was that in case of a real emergency using the fire escape, Mr. Spanks was to carry me down the fire escape so the evacuation could be done quickly and safely.

So the next day Mr. Spanks and I practiced going down the fire escape together so I would know what to expect the next time a fire drill was scheduled. This was the first time I was asked to trust someone outside of my family. For me it was a giant step in learning to interact with others like my Mom and Dad hoped I could.

Besides seeing Mr. Spanks around town, usually on his bicycle, later I'd meet up with him at the Boutwell School during my fifth and sixth grades there. Although there were no fire escape stairs to carry me down since it was a one level building, I knew Mr. Spanks was there. I knew he kept a watchful eye on not only me, but on all the children at the school. He would always help out where and when he could.

It has been almost sixty-five years since I first walked up the steps into Walker School. While the school is gone now, replaced by a state-of-the-art police/fire safety building, the memories of those first few school years are still close to my heart.

The decisions made during those few days in 1957, before inclusion, to accommodate a seven year old girl attending school in a sixty-five year old four-room school house, made a lasting impression on me.

I will forever be grateful to everyone who worked on a simple solution to a problematic issue that no one had foreseen before I was assigned to that school.

Bryan Webster

Here is a simple story, but it's my first memory of Wilmington.

I can remember as a toddler being just old enough to walk to Elia's Market. The original market, of course, before they built where they are now. Every trip there with my mother or grandmother was highlighted with me getting to pick out the shiniest red delicious apple for the ride home. Now as an adult they are my least favorite apple.

My Mother Told Me...
Things We Survived

Contributed by the Group

Our mothers and fathers were wise in their own way as we grew up. The following are samples of their advice, opinions, threats, and pure mean scare tactics to keep us in place. They seem to have worked...for the most part.

Jack Lee *"Keep it up and I'll knock you into the middle of next week."*

Beth Ritchie Pidgeon *"Go out and play."* And, *"Come home when the street lights come on."*

Rose Chase I was brought up by an Italian Grandmother and never knew what she was yelling at me because she yelled in Italian. But I knew enough to just stay out of her way. I do remember she used to always say, *"What goes around comes around."* And, *"Someday someone will do to you what you do to me."*

Cathy Fantasia Seely *"You just wait 'til your father gets home."*

Mary Whitcomb *"You be in by 11:00, nothing good ever happens after that."*

Janet McGinley *"You're a glutton for punishment!"* And, *"Pull yourself up by your bootstraps!"*

Kathleen Bell *"You are going to miss me when I am gone."*

Larz Neilson *"I never heard Philip Buzzell say a bad word about anybody."*

Stephen Gustus If my father heard something he really didn't believe, he'd say, *"I've heard the wind blow before."*

Susan Carlson My grandmother would say, *"I HAVE SPOKEN,"* and we jumped.

Janice McLean Moegelin *"Stop acting like Mickey the Dunce."*

Joyce Noonan *"If your friends jumped off a bridge, would you?"*

Joe Thiel *"Put that stick down, you'll poke your eye out."*

Anne Forrestall My mother advised me to, *"Be careful what you put in writing, because it could come back to haunt you."*

Joyce Eaton Dalton *"How many times do I have to tell you to stop that?"*

Kathy Christensen My mother was a single mom with a backbone and said if we cried, *"I'll give you something to cry about."*

Kathleen Wagstaff *"Mom, my nose is itchy."* And, *"You're going to kiss a fool or have a fight."*

Bob Moore *"Yes, you can lie down in the car beside the rear window!"*

Ann McGaffigan *"Keep frowning like that and your face will freeze that way."*

Don Noonan Dad said, *"Don, you're alright in your own way. But you don't weigh much!"*

Betty Webb *"NOW HEAR THIS!"*

Carol Case *"What would the neighbor think?"*

Mary Lou Govino *"Just because I wear glasses doesn't mean I can't see what you are doing."* And, *"Children should be seen, not heard."* And, *"The best mind our own business."*

Colin Scovil *"I can tell you're lying when your tongue turns black."* My mother used that a lot. Fooled me!

Donna White Simard *"Always wear clean underwear in case you get in an accident."*

Lois Grant *"Why?"* *"Because I said so!!"* And, *"If you get hurt, I'll kill you!"* Also one of mine as a mother, *"You'll miss me, but don't worry, I'm coming back to haunt you!"*

Patti Poloian Park My husband, Lloyd Park, lived on a farm. His mother said, *"If you want to eat supper, you better get out and feed the cows."*

Andrea Aprile *"I am gonna wash your mouth out with soap."*

Janet Witham Hawes *"Make your head, save your heels."* This would be my mother's advice concerning carrying loads of whatever into the house. However, she would also follow up with, *"A lazy man's load,"* if she thought you were trying to carry too much at once.

Tracey Russo Knickle *"He was a tall drink of water."*

Bonnie Eagle *"If you make that face again, it might stay like that."* Also, my father used to tell us if he caught us smoking, he was going to cut a hole in our tongues so we could blow o's! Tell me that didn't scare the hell out of me!!

Deidre Kelley Perrin *"If you say a swear word, the sewing needle* (dragon fly) *will come and sew your lips shut!"* Also, *"You are what your friends are."*

Joann Lucas *"You know I have eyes in the back of my head so I can see everything you do."*

George Keith My brother and I would be fighting in the back seat and mom could drive the car with one hand and beat the hell out of us while yelling, *"Stop hitting each other, you sons of bitches,"* which we thought was funny 'cause we were her sons.

Jack Lee As my old friend Terry Quinlan used to say, *"I'll hit you with so many lefts, you'll be begging for a right."*

Jim Hachey *"Keep it up and I'll give you something to cry about."*

Barry Garden In the middle of January. Mom: *"Will you close that door! We're not heating the town!!!"*

Carol Boisvert *"Look both ways before you cross the street."*

Dottie Pike Lyons My mother used to say, *"You better not talk back to me or I'll knock you into the middle of next week."* Also, my mother used to say to dad if they were arguing, *"You better watch out or there will be a grease spot where you're standing."*

Deborah Shine Harrington Not sure if these were from my grandparents or my folks…but I remember, *"What did you think, I fell off a turnip truck?"* Or, *"Yes, I was born at night, just not last night!"* Safe to assume I was trying to get away with something in both cases.

Diane Clifton If you forgot what you were going to say, my mother would say, *"Must be a lie."*

Alice Anderson Tobiassen *"Close the door, I'm not paying to heat the outside."*

Joe Thiel *"If you strike your Mother, your hand will stick out of your grave."*

Deb Phillips *"Eat your peas, they'll put hair on your chest."* Being a girl, it was not a goal of mine.

Janice Murray While doing something you were told not to, *"If you get hurt, don't come crying to me."*

Jane Woods *"It's all fun and games until somebody takes an eye out."* Or, *"Eat all your supper. There are kids starving in India."* Or, *"Don't go near the swamp. There's quicksand and you get pulled under and die."* And, *"Someday you're going to have a kid just like yourself!"* Also, *"Close the fridge, all the food will go bad."* Last one, *"Because I said so!"*

Donna Murray Follett *"How about a knuckle sandwich?"*

Kathy Burke Fulmer *"You better behave or I will pack your bags to go to the bad kids' house."*

Diana Murray Isqur *"I'm getting the wooden spoon."*

Kimberly Keller *"Shut the door. We don't live in a barn!"*

Becky Dixon *"Go ask your mother!"* Dad says. *"Go ask your father!"* Mom says. Or. *"Do you think money grows on trees?"* And, this from my father. *"You know, when I was I kid I walked three miles to school in the snow!"* My Dad grew up in the south!

Cindy Leathe Kuehl *"If he jumps off a bridge, are you going to jump as well?"*

Synda Anderson *"Your eyes are bigger than your belly."*

Kathleen DelRossi *"You will be judged by the company you keep!"*

William Gustus My mother used to say, *"You're an OMEGON."* To this day I don't know what that is, but I do know it was not a compliment.

Brian Norton *"I'll smack you one."* And, *"Don't talk to your mother like that."*

Linda Aspeslagh *"I'll give you a wallop."* And, both Dad and Mom would say, *"Empty your bladder. If you are in an accident it could burst."*

Stevie Bee *"Don't make me pull this car over...I'll give you something to cry about."*

Gary Carter *"I'm going to wash your mouth out with soap."* And she did more than once.

Ed Carrasco *"Go outside and look for four-leaf clovers. Don't come back in 'til you find one!"* And, *"Do I have to get the belt?"*

Bob Welch *"You had better BE HOME before the 'Horns'* (nine o'clock fire horns) *or the street lights go on...OR ELSE!"* Also from Mom, *"Stick out your tongue to see if you have a black line on it."* (meant you were telling a lie) *"AAA..HAH, there's a black line on your tongue."*

Bernadette Collins From my father, Bernadino Sarchione, *"Do you want me to tune on your head?"*

Jane Loveys *"Get down before you break your neck!"*

Mark Bouvier *"Don't make me get up!!!"*

Trish Jennings *"You dug your grave, now lay in it."* When getting in trouble in high school. And, *"Be home before the drunks get out of the bars." "How can you be late for school when I drop you off at the door ten minutes early?"*

Nancy London *"If you don't stop making that face it'll stick like that"*

Terrijoan Marden Bello *"Don't do as I do, do as I say."* And, *"Don't listen to your father when your mother is speaking."*

Peter Mullarky *"Don't trouble trouble until trouble troubles you."*

Ken Liston *"Billy, Richard, Bobby, Leo, whatever your name is, get over here!"* Also, *"You'd better wipe that smile off your face or I'll wipe it off for ya!"*

Anne Barry *"We don't own stock in the electric company. Shut the damn lights off."*

Bob Wolley I hated peas so much I would do anything to not eat them. I'd feed them to the dog, put them in a napkin, and flush them. My father caught me and whispered in my ear, *"Eat the ffing peas or I am gonna put them in a blender and you will drink them through a straw."* There was a lot of profanity. My mother put an end to the insanity, and other than a few accidental eating of them, I have not had a pea since.

Lauren Turner-Cigna *"I don't know is not an answer."* Or, *"I don't care who started it, but I know who's going to finish it!"*

Ken Liston *"Put down that stick! You're gonna poke somebody's eye out!"* Shouted at me while playing cops and robbers on bikes.

Robin Anderson Downs *"Go play in traffic."*

Gail Ciardi *"If you eat everything on your plate, you can have dessert."* And, *"If you can't say anything nice about somebody, don't say anything at all!"*

Dolly Muir-Pierce *"If you want dessert, then you have to finish your meal and turn your plate upside down."*

Robin Woodland *"Better be home when the street lights go on."* I remember hearing this so many times and racing home because we saw dad's car out looking for us. We actually beat him home a couple times too.

Shannan Turner Cassidy *"Tell me who you go with and I'll tell you what you are."* And, *"I'm not feeding the neighborhood."*

Tori Larkin *"Birds of a feather flock together."*

Janice Ritchie Taylor *"Eat over your plate please."*

Cindi Richards Stratton The classic, *"When I was a kid..."*

Bill Trites *"Put that in your pipe and smoke it."*

Doris O'Connell *"Tie your shoe lacings or you'll fall and break your neck."*

Sandra Enos Conwell My Mom always said. *"Oh, the tangled web we weave when first we practice to deceive."* Or, another one. *"Never put off to tomorrow what you can do today."*

Ted McKie Madelyn used to say, *"I always know where you are."* And she did, after being in the Town Crier as a selectwoman and member of the finance committee and planning board. Everyone knew her and her car, which she handed down to me. One day I slid through a yellow-red light at Wildwood Street near AVCO three miles from home. She already knew when I got home!

Karen Oteri *"I have eyes in the back of my head."*

Gail Donovan *"Two wrongs don't make a right!"*

Steve Brown *"Elbows off the table."* And, *"That is not how you hold a fork. You eat food, not shovel it."*

Lisa Kennedy Cox My mother told me, *"Do unto others as you would have done unto you."*

AnnMarie Barry Legg *"One more word comes out of your mouth…"* Or, *"Is your homework done?"* And, *"Are you complaining?"* And of course, *"WHEN I WAS A LITTLE GIRL, the only toy I had was a doll and a doll carriage made from a cigar box with a string."* Really?

Denise LaRivee Pivarnik *"This isn't a restaurant, you eat what is cooked."*

Michelle Lee When something happened and my parents asked who did it, we all used to say *"Not me!"* My father would reply, *"Who's not me? Does he live in this house? I don't think he lives here, so it was definitely one of you!"* Also, my Mom and Dad (Marie and Bob Woodland) had eleven children. Every night before we shut the door to leave for the night my Mom would say, *"Good night and God bless you."*

Mary Olshaw-Hynes has an oldie but goodie. *"I walked to school up hill both ways in the snow."*

Bryan Davey *"Oh dear, bread and beer."*

Bonnie Olson When my mom used your first name and last name together, you knew she meant business.

Douglas Clark *"What's for supper Ma?"* She would always say, *"Wind pudding with air sauce."*

Darlene Dalessio Whitney *"If you don't finish your dinner, you're gonna have it for breakfast."*

Steve Cavanaugh Got to be a member of the CPC (Clean Plate Club). Can't leave any food on your plate at dinner.

Marilyn Thackeray McGrath *"Keep a dime in your pocket in case you need to call for a ride!"*

Susan Lomastro When my sister and I were giggling, Mom would say we should stop it or we'll be going to bed crying. Never happened! Another one was, Mom would say to never put our underwear on inside out or we'll make it rain.

Brian McCue *"Eat the crust, it makes your hair curly."*

Lori Rankin *"Use your head for something besides a hat rack."* Or, *"See you in the funnies."*

Terry Riel The boys got the whoppings and the girls got the car keys when Mom said no.

Fred Shine *"Blow it out your ear!"* And, *"Get IN this house NOW!"* And the most famous one I always got, *"Turn that damn music DOWN!"*

Karen Newcomb Giaquinta *"Red sky at night, sailors' delight. Red sky in the morning, sailors take warning."* And, *"Believe half of what you see, none of what you hear, and part of what you read."*

Susan Carlson My grandmother used to say to me and my sisters, *"I love you more than the tongue can tell."*

Eileen D'Eon Fenick *"Don't swallow your gum, it will clog your bum."*

Paul Davey Whenever I was caught doing something, I'd always ask my mother how she knew. *"A little birdie told me."* Then, this classic. The first time my dad found papers in my wallet, which had fallen out of my pocket, hours later he finally tossed them in front of me on the kitchen table and queried, *"Are you gonna wallpaper your room with these?"*

Bobby Lanzillo *"I brought you into this world and I can take you out."*

Carol Case My husband's Dad would say when he was doing a chore for his father, *"Skip, you have two speeds. Slow and stop."*

Barbara Mahoney My mom would say, *"Don't chew your hair or it will grow in your throat."*

Alice B. Stone *"If you fall out of that tree don't come running to me for help."*

Gary Carter *"Get up and change the channel on the TV,"* or *"Adjust the rabbit ears."* And, *"Everyone pile in the back of the pick-up truck. We're going for a ride."*

Barbara A. Smith *"Wait until your father gets home."* We would laugh because when he got home we were all in bed.

Rick Norton *"Walk down to the store and buy some cigarettes for your grandfather."*

Dotty Bryn *"Lie down with dogs and you will rise up with fleas."*

Jeanne Cariglio Abraham *"You get me so exasperated."*

Linda Hall *"You can fuss and fume and cause all the commotion you want...but it won't change a thing."*

Mimi McCabe McHugh *"You better tell me what you did before I hear it from someone else!"*

Tom DeLetter *"You kids are going to send me to the nut house."*

Michael McCoy *"Always bless yourself when you drive by the church."*

Fran McLean Donovan Didn't any parent say something kind or supportive? Like, *"I'm so proud of you."*

Ed Patenaude Sr. I can relate to most of the comments. It's like most of us were all in the same household!

Mary Ann Magee McKeen I think our parents all went to the same school.

Remember when...

...everyone you knew ate spaghetti on Wednesdays

Life at the Lake

By Peggy Speranza

I am a lifelong resident of Wilmington, being born and raised here. I graduated from the 'old' high school, got married here and stayed in town. My children also grew up and graduated from school here.

I can remember so many wonderful memories of growing up in this amazing small town. But, some of my best memories are all about Silver Lake and, of course, Tattersall's.

As kids in the summertime we lived to go swimming. Every summer morning, instead of getting dressed, we put on our bathing suits and headed down to the lake. We were lucky enough that our Aunt Renea rented a house near what is now Rocco's Pier, which was down near the town beach.

My Dad would go off to work, and Mom with all my siblings, Tom, Chuck, Mary, Ann, and Barbara, would walk down the Route 38 sidewalk and go to my Aunt's place for a whole day of swimming and fun. My grandmother lived with my aunt, and she would sneak quarters to us kids. We would then walk to Tattersall's (all by ourselves, imagine that) to get some penny candy.

Back then you could get candy for a single penny. We would press our noses against the glass counter looking for that perfect candy while spying the ones that were three for a penny! Wow! That's how we could get more for our twenty-five cents.

We could buy a Popsicle for five cents or an ice cream cone with two scoops for ten cents. Then we would run back to my Aunt's house with our treasures and have a blast swimming again.

We would pack up around three or four o'clock to make the trek back home before Dad returned from work. Mom would be in the kitchen getting supper ready and we would be outside playing and waiting to be called in. Those were the best of times.

I remember Margaret and Hap were the owners of Tattersall's. Margaret always treated me special because we had the same first name. I felt like those two were a part of our family.

Sometimes my Mom needed milk and bread because we would run out before the weekly shopping event at Market Basket. So, she would give me a whole dollar, and off I went to Tattersall's to get the milk and bread.

And, if you can imagine it, I could buy a pack of cigarettes for Mom (something that would be impossible now). Even after buying all those things I got to keep the ten cents change.

I also remember that if Mom didn't have the money to pay, she'd give me a note to give to Margaret or Hap. The gracious store owners would keep a 'tab' for families they knew in the area. I remember my parents would go to Tat's and pay their grocery bill on payday.

Margaret and Hap were such loving people and treated everyone as family. These are my fondness memories I had as a child living around Silver Lake.

Wilmington High School

By Tony Kissel

I was kind of lucky to have spent six years as a teenager at three different high schools in Massachusetts. Before you judge me as being 'slow,' I'll need to explain myself.

In the 1960s most towns were dealing with large increases in student enrollments and their need to build new schools. When I graduated from sixth grade at the Boutwell School, I was moved up to Wilmington High because of inadequate room at the Junior High.

I remember that first week as a lowly seventh grader roaming the halls of the home of the Wildcats. Of course high school seniors ignored me. Members of the successful football team strode by wearing their cool sweaters with the blue 'W' letter emblazoned on their pockets. And then there were the two Fairfield brothers who were so huge I barely came up to their knees!

I was placed in the 7-5 class, which meant I was fast-tracked and my days of getting easy 'A's would be far and few between. I would always be one year ahead in math and French, which created problems for me when I transferred later on.

My bus driver always had his radio tuned to WMEX. My homeroom teacher read a passage from his Protestant bible to us every morning. And, almost all my teachers were young, single women. Things certainly were 'different' at the high school level.

My favorite teacher was Miss Murphy. She was a small lady but had a lively personality. I found her energy level to be incredible, and enjoyed watching her bounce up and down in glee when one of her students finally got the answer right.

She taught us kids about the stock market, and one day we had to pick a stock as our own using a lottery system. I wanted IBM or Xerox, but they had already been chosen. So, I picked Corning Glass Works.

Twenty-five years later I happened to tour the large Corning manufacturing plant in Elmira, NY, recalling that day years earlier in Wilmington High.

At the school my favorite cafeteria food was mashed potatoes smothered with beef and gravy. I would always pay for seconds. The pizza was pretty good there too.

I loved gym class at the high school with Coach Bellissimo. He was a firm instructor, but he was fair. I remember my favorite activities in the big gymnasium were bombardment and hand hockey using a bruising rubber ball.

One day we climbed the thick ropes which extended from the roof rafters to the floor. A friend of mine had reached the ceiling and then lost his grip. He fell down to the hard wood flooring in a few seconds. His legs were banged up and bright red from the long drop and was rushed to the hospital. I never liked climbing the ropes after that.

My turn for an injury occurred during gymnastics training. I was supposed to run and do a forward flip and land in the sitting position on padded mats. Instead, I ran, caught my sneaker under the mat, and flew through the air, landing in a sprawled position on my chin and left arm.

The fall fractured my arm and I had to have a cast put on it. It was difficult, but I soon learned to write with my right hand (I happen to be a lefty). Somehow after that, due to my broken bone never healing properly, I learned to throw a perfect sinker ball. The really cool thing was my classmates signed my hardened cast and carried my books.

Sometimes awkward things happen when a student's mischief catches up to him years later. Fifteen years after graduation I met my old geography teacher, Mrs. Horwitz, at a private school in Newton, Massachusetts.

I was introduced to her as that school's new science teacher. I couldn't help but blush. Back in Wilmington we students had been horrible to her when she had first taught there. I was certain Mrs. Horwitz had either remembered me in particular or the trouble our classes had given her in general. We did our best to avoid one another after that.

There are two clear memories I still have from my Wilmington High days. I remember the Monday class following the Beatles' first appearance on The Ed Sullivan Show the evening before. That's all we students talked about. Soon some of us wore Beatles' boots, had Beatles' haircuts, and bought Beatles' 45s records.

Then, there was November 22, 1963. I hadn't heard anything about the assassination during the school day. When the bell rang I headed out to the parking lot to my bus for the ride home. Students were running every which way, yelling to friends, and crying for no reason that I could see. Cars zoomed pass me. The bus driver didn't have WMEX on and was listening to the news instead. Nobody said a word.

When I got home I dropped my books in my room, then walked over to turn the TV on in the living room. President John F. Kennedy had been shot and killed. I hardly moved for the next few days. It was a sad time to be a teenager.

Next I moved to Tewksbury in the tenth grade and hated my one year in the new school. I was either in classes with eleventh graders or put in classes with kids who didn't want to learn anything.

My final two years of high school were spent at Somerville High. The teachers were old and the three story building was even older. I must have walked 10,000 steps before lunchtime every morning. My senior class was large with 561 in it.

I have to say that those few years at Wilmington High School always bring back fond memories. Sitting at the back desk in Mr. Gilligan's class. Studying for the PSAT in Miss Bartolotta's class. Rooting for Jackie Bowen to score touchdowns. Trying not to laugh with Ralph Blanco in class. And watching my classmates grow up before my very eyes as they became young adults.

To me they will always be 14 or 15 years old, full of life and smiles and jokes.

The Early Years

Told by Joyce (Eaton) Dalton

In 1933 I was born in North Reading in the house my great-grandfather built. My father had lost his job and the house because of the Great Depression.

We moved to Wilmington to a summer camp at 40 Cottage Street just before the 1938 hurricane. During the hurricane I remember having to stay in the car. After it was over we walked Grove Ave and saw trees down in the water and across the road. One tree which had landed in the lake was torn up by its roots. We used to sit on it.

Our little house did not have a bathroom and there was no running water. We had a hand pump that had to be primed to get water. The kitchen stove was oil fueled and it had a water tank in the back end.

To take a bath in the winter my mother would put a kidney shaped tub up on the kitchen table. If you were the lucky first one, you had fresh water. After that the water was heated with more hot water. In the summertime we took our baths in the lake. We would come home with sand-caked soap.

I watched the Silver Lake School being built right off the beach. I was one of the first students to enter first grade when the school opened.

I remember watching my father shovel snow from the street. As he got to the neighbors' houses they would all pitch in. My mother was pregnant at the time and the snow was deep.

When the sidewalk on Grove Ave. was put in I walked barefoot on it. When I went home my mother was very upset that my feet were dirty and caked with concrete.

When I was in the fourth grade our teacher was Miss. Rogers. She later died in the terrible Cocoanut Grove fire in 1942 down in Boston, along with the Fitzgerald brothers. They were uncles to a classmate of mine.

I remember the fireworks at Silver Lake. Also, a dance hall with its cement floor was still there when the beach was put in that required having beach tags to get in. I used to like getting out of the water and sit on it. But later the town tore the hall down.

I also remember the first drowning at the lake. I was ten years old and teenagers had stolen a boat from the Main Street side of the lake. It was about ten o'clock at night and it was sad.

Later in 1945 we moved again. That time to 80 Main Street. And I still live here in Wilmington.

Apple Blossoms

By Brent Clark

I hardy knew my Dad when I was a little boy. Things were very bad at home until he moved out when I was ten years old.

It wasn't until I was late in my twenties that I drove my old pickup to Derry, N.H. and began a long tenuous process to restoration. I love the Spring (new beginnings), so I wanted to share this little essay I wrote about my Dad and Spring.

One time as I was sitting with my Dad, we talked over a coffee and a piece of pie. He told me about a euphoric experience he had when out for a walk one early afternoon. I admit I took liberty and added my Mom to the imaginary dance, since I always hoped someday they could reconcile with one another.

My Mom and Dad separated when I was a little ten year old boy. Neither one of them ever remarried. I know my Mother still loved my Dad for many years after. I am pretty sure that my Dad still loved my Mom, even though both never pursued reconciliation after Dad sobered through the twelve step program. I wrote this story to show a possible scenario of their love for one another.

The old man was out for a walk with his aging dog. They walked along a gravel country road. The summer sun was shining in a moving pattern on the ground as its rays made their way through the leaves of the trees. As the two of them walked along, the road turned into a small apple orchard with thick, overgrown grass underfoot.

The man lifted his head and he noticed the apple trees were in blossom. His pace quickened as he noticed that there were fields of dandelions in full bloom as too. A feeling of euphoria overcame him as the bright colors and the overwhelming smell of flowers invaded his senses.

He began smiling and laughing as he began to twirl around. It was quite a sight to see his stiff knees half bent and his feet running a little bit too slow to keep up with his body.

An old time song from his younger days was on his lips as he danced to it. For just a moment, in his heart, he was young again dancing with his young wife. Memories of falling in love flooded his being as one of the most wonderful times in his life.

Slowly he began to realize that he was dreaming and it was only in his mind. He began to weep in thanksgiving for all the years he had with her. His love for her had been deep, and she loved him just the same.

His dance began to slow as the dog barked at something that made a small noise. He wiped his eyes on his sleeve and took a big breath as he gave a sigh. "Come on, boy," he said to the dog. "It's supper time. Let's go home."

As he hobbled down the road he smiled and thought. 'What was I thinking? I can't dance like that anymore.' He shook his head and chuckled at himself.

Copyright by Brent Clark

> **Remember when...**
>
> ...we were told to put tinsel on the Christmas tree one strand at a time

Wilmington's Old Library
Collection of Memories
From the Group

A long, long time ago in the quiet little town of Wilmington there was a place filled with wonder and excitement and vision where young children loved to visit and discover worldly possibilities.

It was a small, nondescript building set across from the Town Common. Kids would walk there from all parts of town. They would ride their bikes or have their parents drop them off at this magical place. They would meet their friends inside the tight confines of the old structure and spend hours dreaming of the 'what if.'

Beyond the simple doorway there was no ice cream or penny candy to entice the town's youths. There was no Internet or computers or videos or televisions or instant photos or social media platforms or chat rooms to distract them.

Perhaps that was a good thing.

There were only books. Just books. It was the old Town Library which opened in 1890 and offered dreams and hopes and wishes and inspiration and knowledge to our town's residents, changing lives over the next eighty years.

"I remember that little library," **Janet Witham Hawes** recalls. *"I remember so well the high school library and Mrs. Erickson, the librarian. Books allowed me to escape and took me to happier places. Mrs. Erickson will always live in my heart as she allowed me to check out books that were supposed to be for the older students. I went to two schools in Wilmington, the Wildwood School, grades one through six, and then onto the high school for grades seven through twelve. At that time Wilmington did not have any intermediate schools. That meant I was exposed to the high school library and all of its books*

when I was a mere seventh grader. And Mrs. Erickson."

The little old library was dear to many students' hearts. *"The library had narrow aisles and the wooden floor boards were uneven,"* **Kathy Boylen** says.

Looking back to years past, **Carol Bender Gaffney** writes, *"I adored that old library! Got my first library card around 1960 when I was about six years old. My favorite section was the animals/nature one. I remember it was out back and there was a little window seat where I could sit and read books like Ernestine the Pig."*

Kathleen Gilligan has some wonderful memories about the place. *"I spent many hours in that library and became a voracious reader. Mrs. Chipman, the librarian, was so kind to me. I loved to hang out in the stacks in the back. I think there was a long table in the front where you could browse your selections. I always took out the max number of books. Occasionally Mrs. Chipman would let me take extras. We were indeed fortunate to have that memorable little room to launch us."*

"Yes, I remember the table and the small room in the back packed with books," **Cheryl Marr** adds.

Karen Farrell remembers as well. *"I'd sit at that giant table by the encyclopedias working on school projects. Spending more time whispering to friends on the other side of the table. It was the only place to go to do research. A very happy, simple time."*

"I recall sitting there doing research also," **Fran McLean Donovan** thinks back. *"That little tiny building held so many books! One summer I read every book about China and Japan. By the time I was in high school I started reading mysteries. I remember they had a limit on the number of books you could take out and those little cards in front of each book reminding you of the date they were due to be returned. They charged pennies a day if your books were late!"*

> Talking about late book fees, **Dave Knight** shares a story. *"When cleaning out my folks' house before my Mom moved out of Wilmington, I found the autobiography I had borrowed from the library back in the fifth grade. I remember so well getting the late notice and being ABSOLUTELY sure I had returned it.*
>
> *"Things went bad for a bit and finally my folks received a letter or phone call about the late book and the money owed. I asked Dad to drive me to the library as I was upset at being unjustly accused, and embarrassed with my folks to boot. The librarian was so sure I would not lie to her*

(which was true, though I was stupid and forgetful at times and have been for a lifetime, but not a liar) that she decided the book must have been misplaced or stolen. I expect one of my brothers had gotten even and hid the book for a while. And I was SO sure I had brought it back."

Betty Woodland Foumier adds, *"I traveled back to that library once a week after school when I was in the seventh grade. I got six books each time and returned them all."*

"My best memory of summer was riding my bike there to pick up more books to read under the maple tree in our front yard," **Carol Freeman Fraser** remembers.

Mary Whitcomb shares her excitement about the welcomed reading spot. *"I also remember that little room! I couldn't wait to get back there with my reading books. I discovered Dr. Seuss back in those days."*

Memories shared evoke even more great memories. *"Ah yes, Mrs. Chipman,"* **Barry Garden** begins. *"She looked like a typical librarian with an owlish face and glasses. She was wonderful. As I recall, she drove a VW in the '60s and would pull it up on the sidewalk in front of the building. She would close the library everyday for lunch hour. Since I lived next door* to Saint Thomas Church I would walk down to the library or ride my bike.

"If you were looking for your friends all you had to do was look at the bicycles leaning against the chain link fence in front of the building to know if they were in there. Up until the time when the town repaved the sidewalk there, you could see little holes in the hot top by the fence. They were from the kickstands on the bikes that sunk in the tar on a hot summer day. Amazing the little things you remember."

No doubt the librarian Mrs. Chipman had made an impact on area residents, particularly the young readers. **Merrill Poloian** reminisces, *"I actually worked in that small library when I was in high school. Mrs. Chipman lived next door to us on Andover Street. The building was so small and cozy really. I think I read every book in there and used to carry home armloads every week."*

Linda Aspeslagh shares a memory. *"That was my first job in high school. I remember well putting the books back on the shelves, and to this day remember many of the titles and authors."*

"My friend Justine worked there. She got paid $1.15 an hour!" **Sydna Anderson** says.

"When I worked there, I got 66 cents an hour! And my grandmother was a former librarian in that little building," **Nancy London** recalls.

"It was a great place and Mrs. Chipman was a very nice woman," **Paul Bielecki** remembers. *"The first book I took out was a biography on Dwight Eisenhower. I also read the complete set of Samuel Morrison's Naval History of WW2. Spending time in that library taught many of us how to actually do research and get into other factions of life through reading. Back in those days Wilmington had some limitations on what you might do, especially in the winter."*

"What a wonderful place it was. Warm, cozy and inviting," **Judith Condrey Palm** adds.

Great memories and fading nostalgia are often renewed through pleasant visions of the past. **Janet M. Beyer** says, *"That was a wonderful* *little library with its pot bellied stove. It was a refuge in the cold weather."*

Lois Freeland adds, *"I loved that library. Always taking out books, doing homework, using the encyclopedia, meeting my cousin Janet."*

"Back in the day, when I was in college," **Daniel Moegelin** recalls, *"I worked for the town crew during the summer. One summer my assignment in the early evening was to clean the town hall, the superintenden"'s office, and the library. I would usually finish early, so I would sit in the old library reading books."*

Deborah White shares these thoughts about the library. *"I loved that library with its narrow aisles packed with books, its wood floors, and the wonderful smell of books. I learned my love of reading there and still remember some of the stories I read."*

"I loved it. I loved going to the shelf with books for my age," **Kathy Menne** adds. *"My father took me there weekly."*

"I loved it too, but always owed money for overdue books since I took too many at a time," **Maureen Monroe** admits.

Carolyn M. Kenney says, *"I remember the Old Library like it was yesterday. I loved to go there and have loved reading all my life!"*

"I liked reading Edgar Allan Poe, and his books were way up on the high shelves which you had to climb up that ladder to reach," **Ellen EJ Lefavour** says.

"I too remember the old library and being introduced to my first books by a very kind older gentleman," **Peggy Speranza** adds. *"I'm not sure who he was, but I knew he worked there. One of my first books was Harry the Dirty Dog. The old man inspired me to read even though I had a hard time at it. But now it's my favorite thing to do."*

Long time resident, **Charlotte Steward** recalls time spent in the old town library. *"I loved reading. The little library was a magical place. The little room in the back had all the adult books. I was in the sixth grade and Mrs. Ware, the librarian at the time, would let us choose our books. I remember reading a very risqué book when it first arrived at the library. It was A Tree Grows in Brooklyn."*

Harry Landers remembers the old building very well. *"It was part of a perfect pairing with the old Town Hall that stands on the edge of*

Wildwood Cemetery. White wood-frame buildings that say small town New England. Single-story, rectangular, with pitched roofs and minimal ornamentation. Buildings that served the common good of the community, literally separated by the Town Common.

"The library was the smaller sister of the more imposing Congregational church, just a two-minute walk away, going north on Middlesex Avenue. Where, for years, the librarian Clara Chipman was the minister of books. Soft lighting. Hushed voices. The children's section just to the right of the entrance. Were the floors really crooked? Was Mrs. Chipman's desk, right in the middle of the building, her pulpit? The fine cabinetry that held the card catalogues filled with dog-eared index cards.

"And now, the fear, every time I go home, that this building will be gone. Maintenance delayed. No "real" purpose. People with sharp pencils and no sense of history, or shared community, or place will decide that it would cost more to restore the building than it would to just knock it down and build something bigger, shinier, more modern. Because that's the way it goes. It's just a crumby old building. And we need to move forward; not look back. And that will be a sad day."

"One of my fondest memories," **Terry Walden** admits.

Times that are special to us have a truer meaning because of the people we share experiences with. Moments at the beach or football game or library become much more memorable when we are surrounded by people we care for.

Leanne Cummings has a special place in her heart for the old library. *"I remember taking out my first library book there. It was 'Where the Wild Things Are.' I'm not sure what year it was but I think I was in the fourth grade at the Center School right next door. I remember it was really small but I was so excited to be able to take some books home to read."*

"I remember the tiny library," **Kathy Menne** recollects. *"I often went with my father who took out several books per week. I loved going to the kid section to choose something. It was a nice time with my dad."*

"And he continued that with us!" **Charmagne Quenan** says. *"To this day I credit my love of reading to Nana and Papa taking us to the Wilmington Library."*

Carol Case relives those times. *"My dad took us there weekly in the 1950s. He would take out National Geographic magazines along with his books and dream about visiting those 'exotic'* *places he would read about. He was able to fulfill that dream of seeing the world before his passing. All began at that small library and a dream. I also remember Mrs. Chipman and Mrs. Hall. They were so helpful!!"*

Mark Hall relays briefly, *"My mother, Esther Hall, was the librarian in the small building and she would bring us there. I would read books and play Peter and the Wolf, an old record they had at the library. My mother also helped put libraries in the Wilmington schools. She loved her job."*

"I have the same wonderful memories of Mom bringing me there when I was young. I worked there as a page all through high school putting away books," **Nancy Hall Bull** adds.

"My mom did story hours there when I was very young," **Dee Silverman Fransman** shares.

"I loved it when Grandpa Howie and I used to go there," **Brandee Walden Stigman** says.

"I used to visit that library every Thursday afternoon while I waited for my Dad to pick me up on his way home from work," **Linda Kovitch** says. *"I went home with an armload of books every week! I was always excited to delve into*

them once home. It's the reason I still read avidly!"

Larz Neilson always has some interesting information about Wilmington. *"My grandpa, Pete Neilson, was on the library board for about twenty years. He was a mason, so he had no work in the winter. He'd take advantage of his trustee status to borrow a stack of books for his winter reading. My mother worked for fifteen years to build a new library, the one we have now. When the new library opened, her library card number was 007."*

Certain experiences in our lives, particularly when we are young, can lead toward rewarding events in our future. This little old library has changed many people through its stacks of books and caretakers.

"That's where I fell in love with Nancy Drew," **Patty Jaquith Dineen** contributes. *"And maybe why I became an English teacher."*

"I loved that library! Would ride my bike from Hathaway Acres often to see if there were new Nancy Drew books. It took a while, but discovering a new book in the series was cause for celebration!" **Janet McGinley** adds.

Mary Ellen Powers shares a memory. *"I can remember sitting on the floor in the Nancy Drew section almost every day of the summer of '66. It was magical."*

Michelle Lee remembers the early days. *"When I went to UMass Lowell I took a class called The History of New England. We all had to pick one small town in New England to write a history paper about. Of course I chose my hometown of Wilmington and went to the old library every week checking into old archives and looking at old maps to research Wilmington. There was some very interesting stuff found in that room."*

"Loved that small library," **Dave Knight** says. *"It has had a permanent impact on my life. If I hadn't been assigned to the Swain School for sixth grade I may never have gone inside. The biographies were my favorite. I distinctly remember the books about Crazy Horse and Winston Churchill."*

"I remember going there as a small child. I also remember when they moved to the new library. The girl scouts helped move the books over to the new library and one of my sisters got to give a speech at the opening," says **Doreen Case Buckmore**.

Linda Kovitch remembers the move as well. *"I'm also proud to say I participated in the human chain transferring the books to the new library when it was built."*

"I was in that chain too! I loved that little library," **Betty Webb** *recalls.*

John Doucette adds, *"I helped move books from the old library with the Scouts! My father, Robert F. Doucette, and some of the other adults from the troop, also helped. My Dad was a general contractor. Jay-Dee Construction supplied his Ford dump truck to transport the books. We made several loads with care."*

A final thought about the old Wilmington Library. *"I learned my love of reading there. It was a converted one-room schoolhouse, but look at the lives it touched,"* **Larz Neilson** writes.

The SeaBees

NAVY SEABEE VETERANS OF AMERICA
CONSTITUTION ISLAND X-6
WILMINGTON, MA

U.S.S. CONSTITUTION
"OLD IRONSIDES"

Commander/Secretary
Joe Millette
781-665-3037

Senior Vice Commander
Charlie Bevilacqua
781-933-4525

Junior Vice Commander
Arthur Signoriello
617-389-2193

Chaplain
Jim Pedone
781-233-8102

Treasurer
Nick DeCola
781-391-3051

Master At Arms
Joe Francis
978-658-3271

Letter Of Appreciation to:
Joe Francis and his Granddaughter Allison

We the Navy Seabee Veterans of Constitution Island X-6 wish to express our sincere appreciation to Joe Francis and Allison for their CAN DO spirit in helping our Island X-6 become recognized throughout the Wilmington Community.

Through their persistent efforts and a two year long communication with the Wilmington High School Music Department, We finally heard the Navy Seabee Song Played at the Memorial Day Service May 28, 2001. The High School Band played our song "We're The Seabees of the Navy" with much enthusiasm. Our hearts swelled with pride as we silently sang along to our memories. We thank you Joe and Allison.

And Joe our faithful Sergeant at Arms we are grateful for your years of service to the Island and your willingness to help with the crafting of the Island's first Commander's gavel and for the supervising of the repairs to the Old Red School House building. Again we Thank You.

Sincerely your Seabee Friends

After the parades the Seabees marched to the Wilmington cemetery. The band played several military songs, but the Seabees felt left out, so my grandfather and I took some sheet music to the high school and surprised our group.

As the band started to play our music for the first time, the group began to cry and sing from their spots over the grave sites. It was an emotional and very rewarding moment to witness.

I felt very proud. I love our community.

—Alison (Francis) Phaneuf

Classroom Troubles

By Kathy Lawrence Huesgen
WHS Class of 1967

When I was at Wilmington High School I had Mr. Kelley for either pre-algebra or algebra. When he was taking student roll the first day of class I was surprised when he said, "Kathleen Lawrence. Are you related to Al or Gerry Lawrence?"

I replied "Yes" of course, since they were my brothers.

Then Mr. Kelley said, "Get out! I can not deal with another Lawrence in my class."

I almost started crying.

When he saw my reaction, he said, "Okay, just keep your nose clean, don't start any trouble, do your homework and you can stay."

To this day I still don't know what Al and Gerry did to get on his bad side. Looking back though, he was probably just being sarcastic. We were a big family of six going through high school and maybe he was just thinking, "When will this family end?"

~

Then I had an issue with Mr. Nolan, another high school teacher. I lived in the same neighborhood as he and his family. In fact, I was his children's babysitter for many years. Because of that I thought I could get away with murder.

How wrong I was.

I continually talked in his class, passed notes around to my friends, and was being a genuine PIA. So, Mr. Nolan made me stay after school all alone in his classroom.

He went to his guidance office and called my mother explaining the situation. He told my Mom he would give me a ride home since the buses had already gone. Meanwhile, still sitting alone in the room, he got on the intercom and told me, "You like to talk so much, then talk. I want to hear you talking all the time. Don't stop! If you stop talking you will get detention again."

Have you ever tried talking non-stop when you are alone in a big classroom? I couldn't think of a thing to say. When I did stop, I heard over the intercom, "Kathy, I can't hear you. Do you want a week of detention?"

I some how got through it and when I went home I had to deal with even more punishment. Suffice to say, I never misbehaved again.

A Love Song

Shared by Terri Enos Johnston

My dad, Peter Enos, and my mom, Delia, moved to Wilmington from Somerville in June of 1943 with my older sister and brother. Dad loved his new town and raised his family here. I was born that August, lived in town for many years, and graduated from WHS in 1961.

Back in the mid-1950s, St. Thomas church had minstrel shows with local actors and homespun music. My dad, who played the saxophone and clarinet, wrote a song about Wilmington for the shows. The minstrel show band accompanied my dad as he sang his song. The song's lyrics convey how most of us felt about growing up in that wonderful town.

It is with great honor to my family and our dear departed father to share his song with you.

'Wilmington Is My Hometown'

Written and performed by Peter Enos

Wilmington is my hometown.
You couldn't find a better town,
the folks are all so neighborly.
They're like a happy family,
in my hometown.

Wilmington, you'll love I know,
a love that's sure to grow and grow.
Then you'll be feeling like I do,
I know that you'll be saying too,
it's my hometown.

You walk down the street,
and everyone you meet
greets you with a great big smile.

A friendly 'hello', a 'hi' there Joe,
makes your life worthwhile.
Wilmington, I love you so.

And all the dear, dear friends I know,
my heart is here with you to stay.
I'm very proud that I can say,
that Wilmington is my hometown.

Skip and the Gang

As told by Fred 'Skip' Shine

I thought I might share a short story about one of my many antics as a youngster growing up in Wilmington. Some of you know my nick-name back then was 'Skip'.

I got that nickname because I used to skip school a lot and go to Nahant Beach up in Lynn. I'd meet my friends Danny Wentzel, Von Taylor, Tommy Hezlit, and of course, the man with the car, Tommy Gordon. We'd gather in the High School parking lot right off the school bus.

Tommy G had a 1963 Chrysler Imperial. It was a huge blue and white two-tone boat with plenty of room for all of us. We'd jump in our ride and take off, hopefully before Coach Bellissimo would see us leave.

Before getting to the beach we'd have to stop to get something to eat, which if I remember correctly, was usually at Bill & Bob's Roast Beef right off the main road into Nahant.

This one particular day while we were messing around on the beach, I found a sand dollar shell. A crusty sea urchin which looked like a large silver dollar with a star shape on it. Then Danny found one, then Tommy and Von. Suddenly we were all searching for sand dollars in a sort of competition to see who could find the most. There were so many we filled a blanket retrieved from Tommy's trunk.

As usual, we had a good time and returned back home in time to not be noticed as "missing." A week or so later when the weather got much warmer we left school in his car again after class. That afternoon there was this horrible stench coming from the parking lot.

Apparently Tommy had never removed the pile of wrapped sand dollars from the trunk. He picked up the gross smelling blanket of ripe sand dollars and dumped the load into the old swamp near the football field. We almost got caught that time!

~

Another fun time at Nahant Beach, Tommy G had this great "prank idea". If you remember back into late 1966-67, there were gangland style killings in the area where gangsters killed each other and dumped the bodies in Wilmington along I-93.

One body was found in a suitcase, and another one actually lived for a while. Anyway, back then I had a starter's pistol which shot blanks. Tommy had this crazy idea to go to Nahant Beach late one Friday night when all the 'lovers' were parked along the beach watching for submarines.

Tommy stopped at the parking lot entrance. He and Danny W blindfolded me and put me in the trunk of his Chrysler. Then he drove down and parked in the middle of the 'submarine races.'

There he took me out of the trunk and led me down to the beach. Then he fired the starter's pistol, ran back to his car and took off. Earlier he had covered his license plate with a paper bag to prevent from getting caught.

I ran up the beach toward the exit, jumped back into the car, and we took off like the crazy kids we were. As we drove back to the street we saw police cars speeding to the beach.

What in the heck were we thinking back then? If we had pulled such a stupid prank like that nowadays, we'd be in big trouble.

Things We Did

Shared Memories

Many of us grew up in our tiny universe known as the country town of Wilmington. It was filled with new working families looking for a good life. The neighborhoods were tight-knit but scattered throughout the township. And most of them were loaded with energetic, inquisitive kids relying on their own creative resources to get out there and play. Here are some things many of us remember doing back when life was simple and fun.

●Going to the 4th of July festivities, listening to the bands and having pancake breakfast
●Shoveling neighbors' driveways for fifty-cents●Saturday trips to the town dump

●Summer nights rehearsing with the Wilmington Crusaders●Finding the sand bar in the middle of Silver Lake●Pooling change to get enough gas to drive around town

●Relocated city kids learning the country life style●Sitting on the fence up town chatting with Officer Paul Lynch●Plastic bread bags on our feet when wearing ice skates

●Slamming the phone on the receiver in the phone booth when you dropped a dime and got a free call●Walking the paths through the cranberry bogs●The meet-up at Baldwin Steel

> Hearing the fire horns and counting them to find out where the fire was based on the town book that listed the streets by number.

●Watching the parades as a Little Leaguer ●Riding with no seatbelts in the Woodie station wagon●Television stations signing off at 11:00 PM playing the National Anthem

●Going to the packie to buy a byah●Seeing my Collie, Prince, waiting for us at the end of the road after school●The day they announced the Vietnam War was over

●Flying down the pedway on my banana seat bike going 95 mph after school●Helping my brother with his paper route•Hiding the alligator log under bushes at Silver Lake

•Hanging out on Leaky Lane•Taking the driver's test on the Woburn city streets •Sneaking cookies from Mom's secret hiding place in here dresser drawer

•Watching long lines of cars waiting to buy gas on odd and even days•Having neighborhood games•Smearing ten pounds of Bond-O over rotted car fenders

•Winning a real door as a door prize•Hearing the news over the schools' intercom about JFK's assassination•Following the mosquito spray truck on our bikes

•Heading to Winnipesaukee Lake for band camp•Cruising all Friday night on a buck's worth of gas•Mom fixing dungaree knees with iron-on patches to last through the summer

•Clipping baseball cards to bike spokes, transforming our bikes into motorcycles •Fishing for bluegills•Buying one tire at a time for your car

•Setting up a lemonade stand on a hot summer day and drinking all the profits•The

9:00 PM fire horn signaling all is well
●Climbing a tree and too afraid to get down

●Taking the bus to Lowell●Cashing in empty tonic bottles to get enough money for a Bruins' game●Driving up to New Hampshire on a Sunday afternoon to buy beer

●Watching Saturday morning cartoons
●Hiding two friends in the trunk to save two bucks at the drive-in movie●Watching the bonfire at Town Park

●Taking the train to Boston Garden●Having fun at Baby Beach●Playing my favorite music over and over again on the jukebox at St. Thomas Youth Center

●Hitting a tree and getting a bloody nose sledding down Suicide Hill●Going to the dance after the usually COLD game●Working five after-school shifts for a $33 paycheck

●Trick-or-Treating until our pillow cases were full●Checking out the cool muscle cars on the road●Hiding in the woods across from the church until services were over

The Park Family

Shared by Leisa Park

I come from a big family. I mean a really big family. My grandma Dorothy Park and grandpa Philip Park, both who have long passed, had a total of twenty children. There were eleven boys and nine girls, none of which were twins. They are my dear aunts and uncles, and of course, my dad Lloyd, the youngest of the siblings.

Back in the early 1900s my grandparents settled in Wilmington, a small farming town at the time. They lived and the family grew up at the old Ballardvale Street house on fifteen acres until around 1982.

Grandma Park was a kind and generous lady. She was also a hard working woman, which goes without saying, having to care for that many children.

Grandpa Park was a farmer, tradesman, and later, a volunteer fireman. He was a rigid man who believed in strict discipline. Having a strong New England work ethic, Grandpa expected everyone in the family to pull their own weight and be grateful for what they had, even when times were tough. And in those days they certainly were.

Between the two of them, they managed to maintain a strong relationship with the entire family. The family ate well, though many times the supper choices were slim. And they proved to raise a happy family. Although they didn't have very much, what they did have they shared with neighbors and nearby workers and hungry strangers.

Grandma was so resourceful with limited materials and money. She'd make dresses for the girls out of grain sacks. She knitted sweaters and hats and socks for everyone. She made homemade soap, and canned fruits and vegetables picked from their farm.

They sold their share of farm animals they had raised on their land. Cows and turkeys, pigs and chickens. They were the perfect image of tough, self-reliant, independent New Englanders who understood the principles of rugged-individualism and the need of a strong work ethic to survive.

I remember hearing stories from my Dad and the rest about how they lived back then. In the '50s the dozen or so children were packed into a couple small bedrooms. The old house had no heat except for a wood stove. It had no electricity or insulation from the winter cold and wind. Sometimes in the winter, snow was blown through the wall cracks onto the bedroom floors.

It wasn't years later until they had indoor plumbing. The outhouse was set out back and was fitted with three holes, each to accommodate different ages and body sizes.

Dad told me on more than one occasion how he and his brothers and sisters had to walk miles to school and back, barefoot in the snow, uphill both ways! (Sorry, I just had to say that.)

Everyone in the extended family had their chores. The kids tended the fruit trees and garden. They cared for the livestock. They worked on neighboring farms, and cut firewood, and watched over one another.

I heard the older folks talk about how the hard times had made them better people. They had learned the value of hard work, the principles of integrity, the joy of sharing, the peace of their faith in God, and the satisfaction of being able to care for their family.

Grandpa was known to say, "Don't tell us about hard times. We came from nothing and we made something from it."

I am proud to tell you that these people were and are my family. I've seen the good they enveloped pass down through the generations. It's in my Dad and Mom, my brothers and sisters. I hope that I can, too, make them proud of whom I have become.

No Parking

Story shared by Tom Mirisola

While walking along Route 38 with my childhood friends back in the '60s, we came upon a 'No Parking' sign that some motorist had apparently knocked over. So, my buddy Ricky Gray dragged the downed sign home.

After propping it up in his yard for a few days we decided the sign needed a better place where it could be seen. One night our small gang carried the sign through the back neighborhoods down to Silver Lake.

We jammed the sign's bent pole into a log that we frequently used as a raft when swimming in the lake. Then, hanging onto the makeshift barge, we floated it out to the sandbar in the middle of the lake, which was approximately a hundred yards off shore from Grove Ave.

Once finding the small sandbar, which was actually a few feet beneath the water's surface and sometimes a bit difficult to locate, we erected the sign in the rocky pile. The next morning when the sun came up my friends and I were excited to see the shining 'No Parking' sign was visible to anyone traveling the road.

About a week later the local newspaper pictured our 'project' with the caption: "Until further notice, there will be No Parking IN Silver Lake."

The sign remained visible in the middle of Silver Lake throughout that summer and into the fall and winter. When the winter ice was thick and safe we skated around the leaning sign frozen in its unusual place. But when the spring thaw came the shifting ice knocked it over.

I doubt anyone ever retrieved that sign, so to this day it probably remains at the bottom of the lake.

Remember when...

...a dime found under your pillow for a lost tooth made your day

Our Wilmington Teachers
Group Contributions

As young students in our small town we were influenced by many important people watching over us. Our teachers and counselors and coaches had significant impacts on us, not only in school, but also in our personal lives. They guided us in our learning, influenced us in our decision making, and directed us toward our future paths.

We looked up to these educators (well, most of us) in charge of leading and forging us into the world. We respected them, admired them, and even loved them for their efforts, their determination, and their care. Through them we learned kindness and fortitude and confidence. We owe a great deal to these great teachers of our past.

We were blessed to have such great teachers and honor them in these following words.

"Mr. Gilligan was a great science teacher," **Janet Witham Hawes** begins. *"But for me he shone as the best guidance counselor a shy, introverted young girl could ask for. He opened my eyes to college opportunities I didn't know I had."*

Barbara Reinhart-Fitzgerald remembers, *"Mr. Grecoe was one of my favorite teachers. Because of his teaching, when I took my English placement exam at college, I aced it!"*

John Bernard recalls a funny moment in one of his classes. *"My favorite teacher was Mr. Maggio. An endearing memory is a class he taught about Ponce de Leon. He had a little fun with the name which threw my classmate Sven Wilberg into a laughing fit. In turn, he caused the entire class to laugh. I don't recall much of anything else getting done in that class."*

"Mrs. Shea was an English teacher and then the high school librarian in the mid-1970s. She was wonderful," relates **Dee Silverman Fransman.**

Lisa St. Hilaire remembers one particular class period. *"I was telling people about Mr. Fardy from the high school in the '70s. He had the most beautiful calligraphy. We did the coolest things in his class. We actually tested our own blood and urine (pre-HIV, clearly), and learned surgical procedures by castrating rats! We all left that class a little high from the ether."*

Not all the teachers were necessarily remembered for their teaching skills.

"I had Miss Barry in the first grade! One day in class she pulled my tooth out because it was loose. Scared the crap out of everyone!" **Renee Pineau** shares. *"And she had that giant ruler."*

Debbie Donovan remembers, *"That woman was a battle ax. She scared the hell out of me!"*

"Oh yes!" **Sandra Berrigan Fallica** adds. *"She was first grade. I didn't have her as my teacher, but you could hear her! I was next door and just remember all the yelling."*

In every group a handful of teachers seem to stand out.

"Mr. Scanlon was a really great guy! Loved having him as a mentor and teacher," **Linda Kovitch** recalls. *"He also saved my cousin's life. One afternoon my cousin was walking home from school with a bunch of his school chums. They were horsing around and someone shoved him, causing him to fall into the street as a school bus was coming along.*

"My cousin was run over by the bus and his leg was severely injured. Mr. Scanlon saw the accident and ran to the aid of my cousin. He took his necktie and used it as a tourniquet to control the bleeding until the emergency responders got there. Not only a great guy, but someone who

cared enough to help those in need. He's always been a hero in my mind for a lot of reasons."

Barry Garden says, *"The class of 1973 elected Dick Scanlon as the good guy and Carl Olsen as our class advisor for our four years in high school."*

To which **Jack Virtus** responds, *"Which was one of the smarter ideas our class had."*

Nancy Fudge fondly remembers, *"My favorite teacher was Mr. Scanlon. He was the only one who ever called me 'Fudgie'."*

"Mr. Scanlon and Mr. Maggio were my favorite teachers. Mr. Scanlon really understood teenagers and never talked down to us. He was a gem," **Mary Carter** says.

Mr. Kelley, a long term high teacher had his own following as well. *"Mr. Kelley encouraged my daughter to apply to college when she didn't think she would make it,"* **Nana McLean** reminisces. *"But Mr. Kelley helped her."*

"Mr. Kelley was a stickler. Mr. Scanlon was a sweetie," **Shirley Pumfrey** adds.

"I loved both Mr. Kelley and Mr. Scanlon. I have a few funny stories about them too," **Lindsay Currier Hurley** reveals.

Thinking back, **Linda Landry Zwahlen** recalls, *"Mr. Scanlon was a nice guy. We had lots of great teachers at WHS. I also Liked Mr. Desarcina. And Mr. Gilligan had that dry sense of humor."*

Many other Wilmington school teachers are well remembered from back in the day.

"I remember Miss McManus. I was intimidated by her, but she was a good teacher," **Janice Kearney** Fratus adds. *"She challenged me and got me out of my comfort zone."*

Sandra Enos Conwell states, *"I well remember Mr. Cushing. He was our gym teacher 'back then.' Yup, even for the girl students. A story was told that he had some sort of Jeep and in the winter he would drive that thing on frozen Silver Lake to make sure the ice was safe for us to skate on. And happily we skated! And my dear friend Pudgy Cushing was the first on the ice with us. Ahh...the memories!"*

Lois Freeland responds, *"My favorite teacher was Mr. Beaton. My least favorite was the very* *old, bent over Business English teacher and the Shorthand teacher."*

"I loved Mr. Hill for geometry at WHS, Dick Scanlon for psychology, and Mr. Fardy, my favorite biology, A & P, Clinical Practice teacher. We actually operated on live rats in his class!" **Lusann Wishart** remembers.

"Since many of us went from grades 7-12 in the High School, mention should be made of Mr. Nolan, the wonderful guidance counselor and history teacher." **Betsy Walters** adds.

Pam Blais tells of her time in high school and how she dearly cared for her teachers. *"When 9th grade started, I think that was Joyce Aldrich's first year teaching. On the first day we began butting heads, but within a couple months we became best friends. She began picking me up after school and we'd go clothes shopping, then to her apartment in North Andover where she'd cook dinner.*

"I met her husband Gary. I few times I slept over at her place. Loved riding around in her 'Vette, and loved English and how she taught. The last I remember going to visit was to her big beautiful house in Andover, next door to the DeMoulas brothers. I had brought my two oldest children for her to see them when my daughter was a toddler and my son an infant.

> *"I was glad we got in touch a couple of years ago for a few phone calls before she passed on.*
>
> *"During science class I also loved hearing all the memories of Miss Krey and her family escaping the Holocaust and how they made it to America by relying on God's leading them each and every step of the way. That was fascinating to me.*
>
> *"And I thoroughly enjoyed the times in Mr. Kelley's class for in-school suspension. I learned geometry, being in there, but in Mr. Lynch's math class never got algebra, even after being privately tutored and taking Algebra I for two years.*
>
> *"Mr. Lynch let me wash the blackboards to get a barely passing grade in order to not have to take it over again a third time. Finally, I know how to do algebra."*

"They were great. We were very lucky to have nice teachers," **Karen Oteri** concludes.

Getting Around
Trolleys, Trucks, Tricycles, Hikes & Bikes
Written by Larry Gallagher

I recall reading an E.L. Doctorow novel set in the early 1900s. The author described the process of an immigrant father and his daughter leaving their tenement home in Lawrence, Massachusetts and making their way via multiple trolley car rides all the way to Philadelphia.

I was struck by two things. First, that the Northeast at one time enjoyed such a robust public transportation system. And second, that such travel provided a certain amount of freedom for folks of modest means to get from one place to another. For the most part they didn't need to arrange their travel well in advance or adhere to strict schedules or limited routes.

I had this thought that the options the folks have available to move about has significant influence on the culture/lifestyle of a population as it determines the range of activities and geographical boundaries they might pursue.

I contrast the freedom enjoyed by the characters in the novel with the lack of freedom my boys had growing up in Boxford. We lived in that rural community surrounded by trees and some farmland, but we lived on Washington Street, which is also Route 133.

Within days of moving to Boxford I took the boys on a short walk down Washington Street to Benson's Ice Cream, The ice cream shop was a wonderful local institution that attracted patrons from miles away. Without the benefit of sidewalks, and trucks whizzing by at fifty miles per hour, I found myself a few times almost tossing the boys into the shrubs that bordered the road in order to keep them out of harm's way.

And I soon found out that biking along the busy road was equally as dangerous.

So, although we lived 'out in the country', it wasn't safe for my boys, almost throughout the length of their childhood, to leave their home under their own steam. Instead, we had to take them everywhere by car, regardless the activity, whether it be school or school extracurriculars, such as soccer, baseball, theater, music lesson, etc.

We had to follow strict time tables, and one parent or the other had to be available to provide taxi service for these myriad activities, including setting up play dates with their friends. Fortunately, the boys went to an after school program run by the YMCA. That place became their 'neighborhood' of sorts.

I found myself regretting our decision to purchase this particular house, and instead wished we had found a home on a cul-de-sac where my boys could roam the streets (or at least that street) on their own as I had done growing up in Wilmington.

But, I also know that given any number of contributing factors, my sons' generation would never know the freedom, spontaneity, and autonomy that I enjoyed at their age. The basis of that freedom was grounded in our ability to just 'get around'—to go from one place to another. As I think back, the boundaries within which we traveled were far reaching, and in some cases beyond the confines of our small town.

I was born in 1954 and grew up on Cottage Street, now called Muse Ave. It was a small road barely a quarter mile long which ran parallel to Lowell Street and State Route 129. But it was a dead end with minimal auto traffic. It became an extension of my yard and an area in which I could play.

As a four year old I could venture down the street on my tricycle and play with the kids down the end, in this case, my lifelong friend Scott Waugh. This was outside the area in which my mom could maintain visual contact. But so long as I limited my tricycle travels to Cottage Street, all was fine. I also had three older siblings who helped keep watch, or not, as they were not always around.

My friend Scott moved away, but his family returned a couple years later as they purchased a home on Lowell Street whose back yard bordered on mine. We now had an extended back yard in which to play. But of course, we were anxious to expand out territory. We soon started playing with an ever-growing collection of baby boomer children from Parker Street. That became our hangout for the majority of my adolescent and teenage years.

Still, our activities in Wilmington were in no way limited to Parker Street. The whole town of Wilmington became our playground, and so long as we had the wherewithal to walk, or better yet bike, Wilmington became our oyster. The boundaries of our travel increased as we got older, depending on the comfort level of our parents. But back then our parents had confidence that wherever we were, there were other parents who would look after us and help keep us out of harm's way.

I know on Parker Street my mom took great comfort in knowing that there were at least four or five other moms and dads who would step up if we were out of line or in danger of any kind. It does take a village, and Wilmington was a very special village in which to raise children.

My mom worked as a night nurse at St. John's in Lowell while raising six kids with dad. She was forever grateful to George and Mary Foley, and John and Marge Connell, for opening their homes and hearts to the neighborhood kids.

Back to 'getting around'. Our parents made risk-based decisions about what we could and couldn't do. Scott and I were allowed to walk at a very early age (8 or 9) from our house along Route 129 up to Sunnyhurst Farm to get ice cream. We were allowed that freedom because we didn't have to cross Rte 129.

We both had dogs that were hit by cars on Rte 129, so we had a healthy amount of fear and respect for that road. And of course, as we got older, the allowable range of our travel increased significantly, and we walked without complaint to destinations near and far.

Activities we pursued included all things happening at WHS. There were Saturday football games, Punt, Pass, and Kick competitions, events in the Common, parades coming down Main Street to the Center and beyond.

There were Big Joe's Sub shop, Wilmington Center News, Seacraft Sporting Goods, Weinberg's, the Plaza, DeMoulas, Friendly's, Rocco's, and of course , Tattersall's and Silver Lake, which were some three miles away, but all in a day's travel for Wilmington's youth.

And in the other direction we walked to the Wilmington Bowling Alley near the Woburn border. Or we'd go to the Town Park or the Chestnut Street ice rink, wonderfully provided by the Tighes and Waughs and others who generously maintained the rink for the benefit of the town's young folks.

And as you drove the streets of Wilmington you always saw kids walking about. I recall walking home from a football game at WHS and it was like we were part of an after-game parade. There was a steady stream of townspeople walking along Adams, with cars driving by beeping horns and waving blue and white pom-poms, provided of course, the Wildcats won.

Here's another disjointed memory. The price of a student ticket to a WHS home football game was 35¢, which our parents would generally provide. But if there was a way to get into the game without purchasing a ticket, we would always apply those funds to an extra hot dog or hot chocolate.

There were a number of ways to sneak into the game. One was crawling under the fence via trenches that had been hollowed out by some fellow industrious youngsters. These were generally along the visitor's side fence perimeter. But these trenches were often times discovered and filled in.

The alternative method was the Star Spangled Banner (SSB) breach over the much higher fence located behind the home team bleachers. We would wait until the SSB was playing, demanding the undivided attention and respect of the Wilmington police force. That's when we would make our move…scaling the fence as if storming the beaches of Normandy, up and over. Then we would scatter about under the bleachers in all directions before the cops could get a bead on us.

To this day, whenever I hear the SSB played, it seems incomplete if not accompanied by the metallic clatter of a bunch of kids climbing up and over the chain link fences surrounding the WHS playing field on a Saturday afternoon.

'Getting around' continued by bicycle. If you had a bike in Wilmington there was no limit to where it might take you. Little League tryouts and practices where often held on the fields behind the Glen Road School. I lived nearly three miles away but we thought nothing of biking there on a regular basis.

Upon arriving at the school on our bikes we would scoot down that long driveway, and upon reaching the field, disembark from our bikes while they were still moving. Our bikes would glide across the open spaces and then wobble and crash wherever their momentum might finally take them. And we never had any doubt that the bikes would still be there when we returned to retrieve them.

These were bikes with no moving parts except for the chain connecting the pedals to the rear tires. They had one speed, and brakes consisted of simply reversing the pedal motion. We made an art of braking in ways that left large black skid marks on the road.

These bikes were practically indestructible. They were passed down from older to younger siblings, welded from steel tubes designed to withstand the punishment. And they were always there when you needed them. No multi-speed gear mechanism or brakes that needed to be fine tuned or adjusted. In a weird nod to the times in which we lived, we likened our bikes to the Sherman tanks made famous in WWII.

And now finally, to what our parents might have been thinking as we explored Wilmington's byways and countryside. We've all heard accounts that we were allowed to roam free, provided we were home before the street lights came on.

That wasn't the case for me and my friends, primarily because many of the places we hung around, or roads traveled, were not illuminated by street lights. There were stretches of Glen Road or Adams Street that were quite dark, and even a bit scary. But we were undaunted in our desire to go from one place to another. And we did it under our own steam, either in a pair of Keds or atop a beat up old Schwinn.

We didn't give much thought to whatever dangers we might encounter. And for the most part, neither did our parents. We were out and about, doing our own thing, and in most cases we gave them little reason to worry.

Still, I know each night when we returned home from wherever, they felt a sense of calm when they heard our footsteps on the back stairs and then, "Hi Ma, I'm home."

I'm so very grateful that I grew up when I did, and that I did it in Wilmington.

The Right Thing

By Bob Johnson
(Excerpt from *Looking For Eddie*)

One spring day when both my brother Eddie and I were in the military away from home Dad had decided to set up a fruit and vegetable stand at a clearing along the narrow main street near his house.

He knew where to buy the produce wholesale in the city, and for some reason thought he could make his new venture work. This from a man who couldn't even find his way around our small kitchen at Dewey Ave without Mom's help.

We had heard this story told numerous times on the front porch, but he continued his tale. Dad had everything planned out. But there was one problem. He needed to obtain a permit from the town to set up his new business.

So Dad went down to the small Wilmington police station to fill out the necessary forms. The old police chief, Harold 'Slugger' Reed, an ex-baseball player who prided himself in knowing everything that went on in his town, reviewed Dad's application and frowned.

The big country boy said to Dad, "Why should I approve this? I don't know you. I've never even heard of you." He was ready to dismiss Dad's hopes of having a simple neighborhood roadside fruit stand business.

Dad, who lived by the principles he grew up with and instilled into his offspring, stood tall and looked straight into the chief's eyes, two bulls in a standoff, and said, "Why should you approve it? Well, I've lived in this town for over fifteen years and I've raised four sons here. And now you tell me you've never heard of me. That's why you should give me the permit."

The chief stared at Dad for the longest time, then smirked. Without saying another word he nodded, signed the papers and handed them to Dad.

And that, my friends, I'm happy to say, is what the Johnson boys grew up with.

Remember when...

...we carried a load of school books home everyday to do our homework

---

Everyday Fun
Story by Joyce (Eaton) Dalton

I walked to the center of town to do errands for my mother. I also remember going to Tat's for her. They had penny candy out in the open on the counter. A man in the store took a piece, so I did too. A day later my mother marched me to the store and had me apologize.

There was a drug store on Main Street across from Grove Ave. When I had my tonsils taken out, the druggist sent ice cream for me. Unfortunately, I can't remember her name.

We always skated on the frozen lake since I lived so close. There were bonfires too. One time I put my shoes on the deck of a shed. Somebody apparently thought I didn't need them and took my shoes. I had to walk across the street with my skates on.

We would stay outdoors for hours. Any time my mother wanted us home she would put the back light on. When I went to the Center School, we had to walk, even though the bus drove right around our house. All the way from Glen Road to the corner of Grove Ave. After my mother complained, then we were able to catch the bus.

Baby Beach was the best beach on the lake, but now it's closed. I once witnessed a young boy being pushed down in the water by some bullies. He'd get up and then be pushed down again. He finally got out of the water and collapsed on the ground.

When I was in the Buzzell School in the sixth or seventh grade, there was a plane crush. The pilot was flying over his mother's house and hit the ground.

As kids we would walk through the woods from the Buzzell School to Glen Road. There weren't any houses there back then. It was just a path us kids used and is now Drury Lane.

On May Day we'd go to the Common and run around a pole with streamers. When the new high school was built I was a member of the first class to graduate in 1951. Our graduation ceremony was also held in the Common.

The old library is now the July Fourth building. You went down a couple of stairs as you entered. There wasn't much room to turn around in that place.

When I took my driving lessons in school I was very upset when I didn't get my license. Out of twenty-one students I was the only one who didn't pass. The instructor told me he had to flunk somebody. I was a little too far to the left while taking a left turn, and so I was the one.

Two weeks before graduation I met my future husband. We have been married for sixty-eight years now. We have seven children, seventeen grandchildren, fifteen great-grandchildren, and two great-great-grandchildren.

Memories & Changes

Shared by Carolyn Giannotti

I've been in Wilmington since I was four years old. I remember when Wilmington was so much woods. It was very nice back then, but now there are so many stores and too many big houses.

I went to the Mildred Rogers School right near Silver Lake. It was a four-room schoolhouse and we had so much fun playing on the beach area.

I used to walk to school and I'd bring my lunch from home. On the way home I'd go past Tats. I remember all the penny candy. Those were happy, simple times.

My neighborhood in the Dewey Ave area was full of friends. We grew up with block party cookouts and friends who last a lifetime, though some have already left this world.

Living in Wilmington years ago was like living in a dream compared to today. I wouldn't trade the memories for anything.

The four seasons were unreal. Halloween and Christmas were wonderful. Then there was ice skating on the lake and playing in friends' yards. In the summers we went to the lake and played outside all day.

I never left Wilmington and never will, but much has changed through the years.

Nightly Ghosts

As Shared by Margie Campbell

My brother Peter Campbell, who is now a decorated war veteran, shared this story with me from his younger days in Wilmington, and to this day he stands by his account.

On the North Reading edge of town, just off Route 62, is the Wilmington Health Care Center which is part of the Winchester Hospital System. Behind this large building is a health fitness trail that was designed and built in the late 1970s.

The trail was a dirt path which wound through the thick hilly woods. Along the course were designated stations with signs and instructions where runners and hikers could stop, rest, or perform specific exercises.

When the trail was first established many of us walked and jogged the winding route. It also became a hang out spot for many high school kids. Unfortunately, I believe the trail is now overgrown and hasn't been kept up in years.

There were also a large swamp and a twisting creek that ran through those woods. The forest was deep and dark, interspersed with old dirt mounds along the trails. The legend goes that area of the woods was an old Native American burial ground. As young kids we often liked to scare each other by saying the Native spirits would be angry if disturbed.

My brother Peter said that over the years he and his friends would often play in those woods, both day and night. One summer night back in the early 1980s when they were still in high school, Peter and his buddies were playing a form of Hide-and-Seek.

So, on this particular summer evening when the friends started playing, daylight was quickly vanishing as the woods grew darker. One of the teams of friends, including Peter, was walking down one of the trails. About one hundred feet before them, a misty white cloud drifted across the path.

The obscure cloud moved quickly and then shifted like a sheet blowing in the wind. According to Peter they could make out a human-like form within the cloud. The group of kids stopped dead in their tracks, a bit shaken up by the vision. But since remnants of daylight still filtered through the trees, the friends ended up simply laughing it off.

Later that night when it had turned very dark, the groups continued playing their hide and seek game. Peter and his friend Anthony Cutone had separated from their team to hide together. As part of the game the two were trying to 'rescue' other members of their team who had been captured.

Peter and Anthony were walking along the narrow path, moving slowly in the pitch black and attempting to make no noise. As the two friends passed by a section of flat earth further in the woods, Peter said he saw someone sitting on the ground looking back at them.

At first the boys thought it was another one of their friends simply hiding. But this 'person' was not moving. Peter said he moved a little closer to the shadowy image and asked, "What are you doing?"

The 'person' didn't respond, so my brother inched even closer. He noticed that the 'person' was sitting on the ground with her legs crossed, in what we used to refer to as "Indian" style.

The girl had long black hair with two braids on each side of her head. Her elbows were leaning on her knees. Her chin rested on her hands. Even in the fading light Peter noted she was wearing a deerskin dress of some kind with beads on it.

At that point Anthony had moved closer as well and also got a better view of the Indian girl. Peter said the hair on the back of his neck stood up as a cold chill went down his spine. The Native American girl was staring at the two boys with wide open, unblinking eyes.

At that point Peter and Anthony turned and ran as fast as they could down the treacherously dark trail until they found the rest of their friends. The two, still obviously traumatized, told their friends what they had witnessed. They all went back to the spot to see if the girl was still there, but she was gone.

The Real Spirit of Our Small Town
By Tom Mirisola

A childhood memory about growing up in Wilmington that sticks with me was how Rocco Depasquale Sr. helped the community.

Rocco's was a popular Italian restaurant located on Main Street. It was well known for its hearty meals, handmade pizzas, and buckets of spaghetti. Its owner, Rocco himself, was also committed to the town he lived and worked in.

Back in the early days many of the homes around Silver Lake were actually small converted summer cottages reclaimed by young families fleeing the cities. Many still exist today and remind me of those simpler days.

Well, most of those houses had tiny kitchens with small stoves and ovens that couldn't accommodate a large roast, let alone a plump Thanksgiving turkey.

So, knowing many of his customers and neighbors in this close-knit community, Rocco would open his kitchen to local residents, inviting them to bring in their turkeys to cook in his large commercial ovens. When the turkeys were cooked he'd call the residents so they could pick up their holiday main course. It wasn't unusual to see kids walking home pulling their small red wagons with the steaming turkeys.

This was just one of the cooperative spirit stories that made living in small town Wilmington so memorable and special.

~

In the same spirit, as kids, one of our first stops on Halloween night was the side door of Rocco's

Restaurant. We'd yell, "Trick or Treat," and Rocco would give each of us a nice slice of pizza. That's how we began our long night of celebrating Halloween.

By the time we got home, the pillow cases we carried were heavy with candy.

Little Town in the Country

Written by Martha Dimond

My family, five of the eight kids and my parents, moved to Wilmington in 1953. Like many families of that time they wanted to get out of the city. My three older siblings had gone off to establish their lives earlier.

My Dad was born and raised in Quincy and understood city life. Mom was born on a homestead in Oklahoma and was raised in Kansas. Mom had had her fill of city living in the Boston metro, and for her it was time to get back to the land, so to speak.

Apparently, things in the inner city were changing in a negative way, and my parents wanted a healthier and safer environment for us. Before Wilmington, we lived in Washington Elms Housing Project.

I still have memories of our four bedrooms, one bath apartment on the first floor with the piano on the left side as you entered the living room. I remember the little lambs on the pink curtains in the bedroom with my younger sister Cathy.

I also remember riding in the front seat of the flatbed truck that Dad borrowed from my Uncle Bus. That was the night that changed our lives when we moved from the projects to the little town in the country.

I think my parents paid about $500 for our lot of land and tiny 'house' at 35 Park Street. It was actually a one-room cabin which we quickly referred to as "the shack". It measured maybe 10' x 12' with a front window and door.

We kids shared two sets of bunk beds that were attached to the back wall. My parents slept on a roll-away cot. There was a plywood kitchen table that could be collapsed when not in use. The privy was out in the back of the lot. Running water came from a faucet alongside the dirt driveway.

I remember the days of simply playing outside with my older sister. By the time I entered first grade, the town had no kindergarten classes then, we were living in the cinderblock foundation of our home, as were at least some of our neighbors.

It was a beginning.

Our foundation house consisted of 'three' rooms. There was the basement workshop with the coal furnace and workbench where Dad and my brothers got things done. Then the kitchen, furnished with a porcelain sink, a kerosene cook stove, a table and 'cabinets' fashioned out of dynamite boxes salvaged from the construction of Highway 93 just five hundred feet up from our home.

When my mother baked, she would put the finished goods on the cellar window ledge to cool. When we picked enough blueberries from along side the road up on Woburn Street, Mom would make muffins, making us kids feel proud of our contribution.

Our house felt so luxurious after having lived in the cabin. The rest of the space was divided into sleeping areas and a living room.

Eventually we acquired a TV with a tiny little screen. My older brothers and my sister and I would squabble over watching American Band Stand or The Mickey Mouse Club after school.

We also had a big ol' radio standing outside the kitchen area. I remember sitting next to it and listening to radio shows, perhaps soap operas. It was like having a story read to me. The dialogue and sound effects created images in my mind.

In retrospect, those radio shows left more of an impression on my mind than did the TV shows. There was more comfort and pleasure in listening to the radio.

One October morning of my first grade school year, as I stood in front of my mother so she could comb my hair in preparation for school, she asked me, "Do you know what today is?"

I didn't, but Mom told me it was my birthday! Oh my! Did I feel special. I had no expectations of great gifts or grand parties. We didn't celebrate that way.

My birthday was more of an internal, private celebration. But when I got to school I told my teacher. At the end of that day I left school with a stack of birthday drawings made by many of my classmates. They were just for me!

I will always remember that teacher for the simple act of kindness. After school I sat on my bed in that humble cellar with the many drawings on my lap, admiring them one by one and feeling like I meant something to my classmates.

I think it was a feeling of being an individual, not just one of the eight kids in my family or just one member of my class, always a person in a group of something, rarely an individual worth noticing.

Those little drawings have remained in my heart ever since and always come to mind on my birthday.

As for the construction of Highway 93 and its impact on our home, I will quote my mother in her letter sent to one of her brothers back in Kansas. She opens her letter by admitting to being a little homesick after reading a letter from him telling about his activities and wishing that she "could get out there once again to at least spend a summer. But God only knows if I'll ever get to do it."

Any extra money had to go into the building of our house. At the time of this letter, May of 1958, there hadn't been much progress. "Right now," Mom's letter continued, "we don't know what will happen. The new highway is being built and they are taking fifteen feet of our property frontage.

"Our street is going to be built over the new eight-lane highway as they continue construction on the Boston-New Hampshire line. We were told that when the highway was done it would only take twenty minutes into Boston." That was my mother's perspective. For me as a kid, it was far different.

Where the road was being constructed some of my friends and neighbors lived in homes right in its track. My closest childhood friend lived just about where the northbound lanes run now.

The house was probably originally built in the mid-1800s. It was the home of her grandparents, Mr. and Mrs. Chisolm. I knew her grandmother because she watched over the children while their parents worked. My friend's Mom worked at the Post Office and her Dad worked for the Boston & Maine RR.

I remember the grandmother sitting in her corner chair in the living room, knitting away. And, the kitchen had a real pantry! I loved that pantry, even as a kid. It made sense to me.

We often played in her house. At Christmas time I'd visit to check out my friend's presents, which included new dolls, lots of clothes, coloring books and crayons, and game boards.

Outside in her yard there were tall pine trees and a ripe old apple tree. We'd eat the dropped apples which were sweet and tart. It was pure magic to eat apples that simply grew right there in the backyard.

Good Times in the Country
by Beverly O'Connell

I remember the Wilmington Skating Club located on Chestnut Street. I loved going there on the weekends.

Inside the old school, which is now the Wilmington Food Pantry, I think was a wooden interior with wooden benches, coat hooks for hanging wet clothing, and a big pot-bellied stove for heat.

Familiar faces there were Nancy Weinberg, Cookie Cotter, Jeannie Ashworth, and many of the boys on the speed skating teams. The pond we skated on went much farther back than it would appear now. I think it was maintained on a volunteer basis.

Again, familiar faces included the Butlers, the Backmans, and several other families who lived on Chestnut St. Some of the Moms would send along plates of homemade cookies and other treats for us kids. We could see into the night hours fires that were lit and the occasional electrical lightning.

I also remember the place called Snug Harbor located on Burlington Ave., which was owned by the Del Torto family. It was a house with a big old barn, which has since been condemned.

I grew up at 1 Dell Drive. Dell Drive was also owned and developed by Mr. Del Torto. Across the road was a large open field thick with buttercups and daisies and grazing horses. I remember three of the horses' names: Gypsy, Lady, and Major. There were other boarded horses too. It was fun jumping on their backs and riding around on them without saddles or bridles.

We had a very unfortunate and scary incident one day when a young boy who lived next door was kicked in the face by one of the horses. That was a terrible day.

In the woods around the field we built forts. We caught snapping turtles in the pond and took them on a wagon ride. Later we put the turtles back in the pond.

In the springtime we would pick wildflowers and loads of pussy willows. Roberts Road, which was the next road going toward Wilmington Center, was prime blueberry picking with rows and rows of blueberry bushes. We'd pick quarts of blueberries. Then Roberts Road was developed.

Even before we were eight years old we'd walk or ride our bikes to a store down off Route 62 at the corner of Forest Street to buy penny candy or ice cream. At that time we knew the names of every homeowner on both sides of the road.

Wilmington was a really fun small town back in those late '50s and early to mid '60s.

Remember when...
...a Band-aid fixed everything

Hermit in the Woods
As told by Michael Barcellos

Here is a crazy story I recall being told when I was a young boy growing up in Wilmington.

When my grandfather moved to Wilmington in 1955 he bought land on Ballardvale Street before industrial zoning and development took over the area. It was a lonely country road dotted with a few houses with RFD addresses. The road connected Route 125 to Lowell Junction and the small Andover hamlet of 'Ballardvale.'

When my sister, who is eleven years older than I, and my cousin who lived next door, started school they needed to walk quite a ways down the street to catch the bus. The problem was that they encountered chilling snarling and barking from the woods when walking to the bus or coming home.

My parents and aunt and uncle complained to the school about the dangerous situation. Eventually the school bus came farther down the street right at the Andover border. But the local families still heard the dogs in the woods. At night the animals would come out and howl viciously and chase cars traveling by.

The rumor was the dogs 'belonged' to a 'hermit' who lived in a shack in the woods. Apparently he fed them when he could, but the animals were wild and unapproachable.

So, my father and uncle, who both had served in WWII and had extensive weapons training, went to Sears and Roebuck and bought bolt action 410 gauge shot guns.

The two men rode up and down Ballardvale near where the pack of wild dogs charged moving cars. When the fierce animals came out of the woods and attacked, my dad and uncle shot them.

The physical proof that those dangerous dogs actually roamed the neighborhood was evident. The Animal Control officers came out and gathered up a bunch of orphaned pups that were also vicious and unapproachable.

When the police attempted to find and contact the hermit, apparently he hadn't fed his dogs that well. All that was left of him was his bones.

Again, this is from stories my Mom and Dad, my Aunt and Uncle told us kids back in the 'good old days'.

Days in Early Wilmington

As Told to Charlen Landry

These reminisces are from our sister Emily (Terri). Our family moved to Wilmington in 1945 after Dad came home from the war, and Emily, our older sister, was only two years old.

Their first year in town they lived in a summer cottage on Dobson Street, which was owned by an aunt and uncle. During that year dad was busy building our first of three houses one road over on Fay Street near Glen Road.

The only heat in the small house was from the kitchen stove, so Mom baked a lot. She also stuffed newspapers under the mattress and on the floor in Emily's room to afford some degree of insulation from the bitter cold.

Emily attended Mildred H. Rogers School right along Silver Lake. She said that if you were signed up for lunches, you ate whatever they served that day, including corn chowder (which she likes now but did not then).

She recalls that she and any kid who had ice skates would bring them to school. After school was out they would skate on the frozen lake until it was time to take them off and race home to Fay Street before dark.

Mildred H. Rogers School taught grades one through four. Grades five and six were at the Buzzell School which later was turned into an elementary school for grades one to three. After school, if any of the kids were lucky enough to have a few pennies or even a whole nickel, they would go to Tattersall's to buy candy or maybe an ice cream.

Emily told Charlen that she remembers what she thinks were Christmas trees after the holiday being burned in bonfires on Silver Lake. Heavy town fire trucks were driven onto the lake's thick ice to make sure it was solid enough for skating and pick-up hockey games. Sometimes our Dad participated in the ice games.

My sister also remembers that back then every town household had a list of the town's fire codes which indicated the location of fires. This may have been as a result of Wilmington having a largely volunteer fire department. The fire horn would automatically blow at 9 A.M. and 9 P.M. and just about everyone in town could hear it.

These are some of the memories of growing up in Wilmington in the latter years of the 1940s and early 1950s as dictated to me by my sister Emily.

Clyde McKaba

In 1964-65, me and a couple of friends went out and painted ¼ mile stripes across a few roads in Wilmington. One was Concord Street. A couple of times I took my Top Fuel Dragster over to Concord Street and push started it to make sure everything was okay before heading to the track.

A Tribute to Robert Parent
Fallen Heroes: Part III
By Fred Shine

Sgt. Robert Warren Parent served as a helicopter side gunner with the 101st Airborne Brigade. He was awarded the Air Medal with oak leaf clusters. "Bobby" was killed in his thirty-fifth helicopter combat mission in Vietnam in 1968.

Parent's monument was a difficult search to find a special place. His parents had sold their house in Wilmington and moved to Florida. I did not know Bobby as well as Jackie Fullerton or Richard Welch, so I didn't know his friends or who else to reach out to for information. So I used my imagination in finding an appropriate site.

When we were growing up, Wilmington had a Town Hall next to the Wildwood Cemetery which was moved to the old Glen Road School building. The old town hall structure was proposed to become the Wilmington Historical Building.

My thoughts were, "What an excellent place to be remembered. Also, the building sat higher on a small hill overlooking the cemetery and the "Field of Crosses" where Bobby and other military heroes are laid to rest. Well, since Bobby liked to fly and sort of 'look over and protect,' I thought this would be a perfect spot. He would be looking over the others he had served with.

At first everything fell into place without any problems until I had planned the actual dedication. The bronze plaque factory went on strike and I had no connections to make a temporary plaque. Unfortunately, I was forced to postpone the dedication.

Bobby's parents came to Wilmington that summer for a vacation and I made plans for the ceremony since I thought it important for them to be there. But, since the plaque was on hold, they flew back home. Not a week later and the bronze factory reopened and shipped the plaque.

I contacted Bobby's parents to find out when they planned to visit again and they told me they couldn't return until the next summer because of the expense. His Mom told me they appreciated my efforts and to just go ahead with my plans.

Well, that just wasn't going to happen. I wouldn't dedicate a memorial to their son without them being there. So, my brain started to grind! I called United Airlines and explained the situation. I asked if they would be willing to make a donation and fly Bobby's parents here free of charge for the dedication.

I was informed I needed to write a letter and send it to them so they could review it and forward it to their corporate office for approval. I was also told "it would take some time."

So, as I pondered how to write the request, bearing in mind that I wasn't really a good writer, but I was a good talker, it took a few moments to gather my thoughts.

As I began writing, my phone rang. It was the man from United Airlines who I had spoken with. He said, "Well, I'm sure this will get back to you, so you may as well hear it from me. After we spoke," he continued, "I made a statement in the office to some of my associates. 'Some guy wants us to donate tickets to get his friend's parents to their son's dedication for a Vietnam Veterans Memorial in Wilmington, Mass!'"

Well, as luck would have it, Betsy Costello, who grew up directly across from my house on Cottage Street, worked in that very office. After hearing the story she yelled, "That's Freddy Shine, my old neighbor! He's been doing monuments for four boys killed over six years, fighting all the way!"

Apparently, the man I spoke to said, "Without any delay I approve two First Class roundtrip tickets and will arrange to have a limousine pick them up at home and return them back home afterwards!"

Bobby's parents would be here for the dedication. Excellent! Now I needed a place for them to stay. They had a son, Tommy, who lived in Nashua, NH. But he had a small house and didn't have a spare bedroom.

So, I made another phone call. I called the Sheraton Tara in Nashua and explained what was going on. They immediately gave me a free room for Bobby's parents. Everything was now in place. The ceremony was on again. Bobby's parents and family were there and the dedication was a great success. To this day I remain friends with Tommy and see him from time to time.

Now, I only have one more memorial to build, John Allen Rich, USMC, the first man killed from Wilmington in Vietnam. His story is next. It is both a complicated and unfortunately very true and sad piece of history, and should never have happened!

Schools We Knew
Past Students

We all had to go to school, and considering that, most of us still turned out pretty good. The 3-Rs were our basic education and we still know our multiplication tables. We learned what we needed and had a well rounded foundation to take us into the future. But not all learning came from the classrooms. Here's what past town students have to say about the schools they knew well.

- Learned how to hide in the woods from the truant officer•Watched Saturday morning movies at the High School auditorium•Fell asleep in my algebra class

- Got bussed from my elementary school to the High School to get pickle juice on our teeth•8th grade trip to Niagara Falls with Mr. Bill Peabody•Trying not to get a wedgie in those gym uniforms

●Cruising through the H.S. parking lot by the tennis courts to see who was out and up to some shenanigans●Listening to the jukebox in the old high school cafeteria●Detention in the principal's office

●Missing the school bus on purpose, then walking to Dunkin's for breakfast●Walking to the cafeteria, high from ether from operating on Mr. Fardi's rats●Failing an English test!

●Practicing 'The Hustle' while waiting for the bus at North Intermediate School●Skipping the fire drills by hiding behind the auditorium curtains●Working in the cafeteria to eat free

●Skipping homeroom to hang out with my boyfriend●Smoking in the boy's room●First four grades at Mildred Rogers School with recess on the beach

●Getting smacked on the hand with the teacher's ruler●Climbing from the High School roof through the bathroom window off the gym to get into the 1972 dance●Hallway fights

●Running through the maze of bushes on the hill between the Buzzell and Swain Schools at recess●Trying your best to climb the rope in gym class to tap the roof rafter●Forgetting your hallway pass

●Honoring the U.S. flag in homeroom
●Having an extra nickel for a second piece of double chocolate cake in the cafeteria●Giving up on how to figure out how a slide rule works

●Listening to the class song, 'Bottles of Wine,' over the homeroom intercom●Hiding under our desks after the siren sounds●Taking French class because the teacher was 'hot'

●In the little red school house (West School) where half the class was first grade and the other half was second grade●Missing school to spend a day in Boston●Faking a letter of absence from your mother

●Listening to the 1967 World Series over the school intercom●Giving the new substitute teachers a hard time●Hiding 'stuff' in your school locker

●Walking in the opposite direction of your school in order to take the bus●Steering clear of the 'troublemakers' in the hallway
●Praying for one more snow day

●4th grade class in the cafeteria at the

overcrowded Woburn Street School●Carrying a load of text books home for homework
●Having to take summer school classes

●The solemn quiet in the high school the day after JFK was shot●Cramming for your finals
●Caught cheating on a chemistry test

Polliwogs and Oil Barrels

Shared by Christine Jillett

I grew up in our house right across from Silver Lake. There was a brook that ran along part of Main Street and twisted behind my house as it drained into the lake.

As kids we played in that running creek all the time. The rocks and pebbles in the water were slippery and slimy from the constant current. In the spring time we collected wiggly little polliwogs from the creek's edges after they had separated from the jelly-like clumps of new eggs.

We'd carefully place the tadpoles in a jar of water and marvel at the baby frogs with their tails and protruding back legs. After a few days we would return them back to their home so they could grow into full size frogs.

Another fun thing I did with my brothers was rolling giant old oil drums. The dirty, rusty barrels were abandoned by a local gas station not far from our house and were left in the woods. My brothers and I would get on top of the drums and roll toward each other like professional log rollers.

We rode those tanks as if they were bumper cars. We crashed into one another, fell off pretty often, and laughed until we could hear our mother screaming our names to come home.

It was our form of fun and it's a wonder none of us got hurt!!

Remember when...

...everyone in the class got a Valentine's card

Teachers Teaching

Stories shared by Charles Fleming

I have many memories about growing up in the small town of Wilmington. My first day of school was at the Buzzell School. Mrs. O'Keefe was my teacher. My mother and her friend Ruthy took me and her son David to our classroom.

Mrs. O'Keefe got my attention by showing us boys how to write our names and tape them on the corner of the desks we were assigned. I turned around to show my mother and she was gone! I got up and ran out of the building, making it to the nearby Swain School before I was found.

Remember, all of the teachers at the school were not that young. I didn't know where I was going, but I was on the move. Mrs. Kennedy and Mrs. O'Keefe finally caught up to me.

Mrs. O'Keefe was a teacher who treated us kids with much kindness. I enjoyed my year with her. She was actually responsible for me getting promoted to the next grade.

My mother was not well for most of that year, and my teacher filled in areas of my life by giving me extra attention when I needed it. I'm glad to say that my mother eventually got better, but I thank Mrs. O'Keefe for her caring and help. I still remember her as if it happened recently, but it was sixty-four years ago! How time flies.

~

As young children our teachers impacted our lives.

I remember in Mrs. Donahue's third grade class having to practice learning how to write. A very lovely older woman would conduct a class teaching the class how to form letters. She was especially good at Capital letters. She made them much fancier than usual.

Another memory which sticks with me is my fourth grade teacher, Joan Myers. I think it was her first year teaching. She was strict, but not mean.

Many years after I graduated from high school I had the opportunity of meeting her. The first thing she said to me was that she remembered my penmanship skills. I guess she liked the way I wrote.

In fifth grade I had Mrs. Scully. She was the principal of the Glen Road School. She was also the director of the Glee Club which I joined. I remember having some art work posted in the front of the classroom that I had painted with water colors on heavy construction paper. She must have liked it enough to hang it along with others in the class.

Then in the sixth grade I had Mr. Gagnon, also at Glen Road School. I remember he used to smoke a pipe. He started a camera club, and on Saturday mornings he would hold classes on how to take pictures and how to develop them. We used the bathrooms in the school as dark rooms since there were no windows.

Mr. Gagnon once had a skating party at his home on Crystal Lake in Chelmsford, including a winter cookout for members of the camera club. He was a great person.

Near and Dear to my Heart

By Christine Jillett

He would pick me up almost every day. He lived near the lake too, so it was easy. David picked me up on his bicycle, which was almost too small for him.

We were young and he was my friend.

I would hop on the handle bars and off we'd go on some adventure. There was a lot to explore near and around the lake. We would go up and down the side streets. We'd ride through the pristine hay fields stirring up the grasshoppers. We'd ride through forbidden areas, laughing together all the while.

We often stopped at Tattersall's for ice cream or candy, and then rode across the street to Baby Beach. We would take a dip, jump off the wooden raft anchored just beyond the beach, maybe sit in the sand to soak up the warm sun. Usually our final stop was at my house where we'd listen to records and play fighting or wrestling.

One time when we were wrestling, David kissed me! We were both shocked. I don't really recall what happened after that.

That kiss was the end of our childhood play. I didn't see David in school much after that. I heard some time back that he died while riding his snowmobile up north.

A child on a bicycle...an adult on a snowmobile. Always seeking adventure. R.I.P. David.

THE LANDERS FIRE
by Janis Jaquith

On September 26, 1969, a fire took the lives of a mother and five of her children.

It was after midnight, and all eleven people in the Landers house on Clark Street were asleep: Dave and Nancy Landers, their eight children, and Dave's cousin Joe Casey.

In his first-floor bedroom, a winterized former porch, Joe was awakened by intense heat and bright flames through the glass door that connected his room to the den. Hoping to wake up the family and lead them to safety, he opened that door and encountered a gust of heat and flames.

In that brief moment, Joe beheld an odd sight. Instead of seeing the den wall, he could see all the way to the front of the house. Panicked and with a badly burned hand, he broke a bedroom window and climbed outside.

There was a BOOM that woke up Nancy Landers and her husband Dave. At first, they thought it was an earthquake. The tongue of flames visible out their second-story window told another story. They rushed to one of the two children's bedrooms upstairs, the one with their three daughters: 4-year-old Kathleen, 7-year-old Lisa, and 14-year-old Susan. They opened up a window where Dave took his place standing on the small roof below, ready to lower the girls to safety. Susan was first and jumped down to the ground. But the opened window had instantly pulled the furnace-like heat and smoke up the stairs and into the bedroom.

Overcome by the heat and smoke, Nancy was unable to lead the two younger girls to the window. Dave tried again and again to enter that furnace, but succeeded only in severely burning his skin and lungs.

In their basement bedroom, teenagers Mike and Harry woke up to the house shaking and feared the oil burner was about to blow up. They escaped through the cellar door.

Someone called for help. It may be that the person dialed O for Operator (a common practice in an emergency at the time) rather than find and dial the number for the Wilmington Fire Department. This was before the 911 system.

There was a substantial delay in the WFD response. It may well be that the operator, who would have been in Malden, misdirected the call for help to another town with a Clark Street. The moment the WFD actually did receive a call from another neighbor, they were out the door and on the way.

Meanwhile, neighbors were running garden hoses from their houses to the Landers' house, and reported hearing Dave, still up on that small roof outside the window, desperately screaming Nancy's name, again and again.

By the time the firefighters arrived, it was too late. Too late for Nancy and her five children. The two girls were found on the floor a few feet from safety, their mother's arms around them. The three boys, Kevin, 9; Billy, 11; and Davey, 13, were found in their beds, mouths and nostrils ringed with smoke.

In 1969, the fire was labeled "electrical"—a catch-all phrase, back then, which often meant "we don't know."

Shortly after the fire, a young man allegedly bragged to someone that he had started it. Police interviewed Susan to determine whether that man had shown any romantic interest in her. She knew him, as did others in the family, but there had been no romantic interest. Police spoke to no one else in the family to determine whether this had been a set fire.

Additionally, in the months following the destruction of their house, when the family was living in a trailer in their back yard, someone set a fire under the trailer, using newspapers and kerosene, attempting to set fire to it as the survivors slept inside.

Fast forward to 2011, when I, with encouragement from my Landers in-laws, set out to find out how that fire started. The fire chief at the time, Ed Bradbury, agreed to meet with me. He'd unearthed a set of photographs taken inside the house just hours after the fire was put out. He spread out the pictures on his desk and pointed to the details that jumped out at him as indicating a set fire. The most obvious were the two points of ignition. If it's arson, the arsonist will often start the fire in more than one spot to ensure success.

Bradbury and Wilmington Police Department detective Chris Neville were part of the ensuing effort to uncover connections between the person of interest who allegedly confessed to having set the fire and the fire itself.

When interviewed about the renewed interest in the 1969 fire by *The Boston Globe* in a video that appeared on boston.com in 2013, Chief Bradbury said that there appeared to have been both a motive and an opportunity, declaring, "At the end of the day, my feeling is that Nancy and her five kids were murdered."

It appears that there were no eyewitnesses, and no one has come forward with testimony or further evidence that could bring the guilty party to justice.

But now, after all these years, we are certain that this was no electrical fire. It was arson.

Author's note: I've been married to Harry Landers since 1976. I grew up on Dorothy Ave. near the North Intermediate School. WHS Class of 1970, both of us.

Back to School

Shared by Donna White Simard

I had left Wilmington High School in my 1966-1967 senior year. I got married at a young age and we had two children. When they both started school, one in Swain School and one in St. Thomas kindergarten, I decided I wanted to get my high school diploma. I was twenty-five by then.

I went to the high school, and Mr. Cogan was the guidance counselor. I thought I would have to go to night school or something, but I was wrong. He suggested I go on a work study program. He told me my job, beside my studies, would be taking care of my children. So he arranged for my youngest son to attend morning kindergarten all year long.

By that time, my best friend still to this day, Martha Land Boudreau, was teaching at the high school. Going back to school at my age was different. I could even wear jeans! Anyway, I had to take three classes. I had Miss Helmer for Children's Literature. She was actually one of my teachers when I was still in high school. I also had Mr. Shea for Accounting. This many years later I unfortunately forget who my third teacher was.

None of the other students knew I was married and had children until one day in Miss Helmer's class. We were discussing a book when the teacher matter-of-factly said to her class, "Do you know Donna is married and has two children of her own?"

Of course, everyone turned around and looked at me, but they were all so awesome and had lots of questions. Mr. Shea's class also found out my open secret.

The students were great. You know how fast students can put things out! They all took me under their wings. They begged me to go to graduation with them. I still have their class pictures.

So anyway, I did go to graduation at the age of twenty-six. My parents, in-laws, husband, and children where there too.

This all happened, which changed my life, because of those teachers. Oh, and Miss Helmer gave me the longevity award!! Later, I went on to work as a secretary at a high school in the Guidance Office and in the front office for a principal for ten years.

I do have my diploma from Wilmington High School. It says Donna Simard instead of Donna White, and 1975 instead of 1967, but I got it!!

Remember when we had license plates on our bicycles? I saved my plate from my Columbia Bike that's now long gone. We got the plates from the town hall and they were supposed to help the police reunite our bikes with their owners in case they were stolen or lost.

It was originally green with white lettering, just like the Mass auto plates of the early 1960s. I sanded off the rust and repainted it Wilmington royal blue and it's now mounted on my golf cart in Florida. Tom Mirisola

---

A Look at Early Wilmington

Shared by Elaine DePasquale

Wilmington was a small town when I first visited my Aunt Theresa's house at 835 Main Street. I was only five years old at the time.

When my cousin and I grew older she went to the Mildred H. Rogers School near Town Beach. Since I didn't live in town then, I went as her guest for the day. The school had been named the Silver Lake Elementary School for some years.

Years later I heard that the school was renamed after Mildred Rogers, the principal of the small building, who died in the Cocoanut Grove tragedy in 1942, one of the worst fires in Boston history.

My Uncle Charlie would drop us off at the Wilmington Theatre on Main Street in the center of town. We were typical young girls and we'd run to the ladies room and put on lipstick. We made sure to wipe it off before my uncle came back to pick us up.

Later still, I moved in permanently with my Aunt and Uncle Charlie and my cousins.

In 1961 I graduated from Wilmington High School and got a job at Rocco's restaurant. That's where I met a young man, Sal DePasquale. Then we were married.

Sal and I raised our four children on Jacquith Road, not far from the restaurant. My son Rusty still lives there in the very same house he grew up in. Now I live in elderly housing in Chelmsford, but Wilmington will always be home.

Remember when...

...Halloween was a chase to collect the most candy bars possible

Old Friends

Shared by Chuck Burns

Remembering my childhood/teen years friends from Wilmington, Massachusetts.

As many of you may know, I've traveled the country and world fairly extensively. But one thing that has struck me and stayed in my mind was how far and widely spread my friends were, and how many of you I've encountered in far away places.

First encounter was with Winston Fairfield who was playing basketball for Indiana while I was attending the University of Michigan. We had a pleasant exchange after the game.

Then I ran into Claire Graham in 1966 on Waikiki Beach, Honolulu. We had a fun time reminiscing.

A few years later I had a pleasant chat on the sidewalks of Washington, DC, with Lucy Keough. A couple of years later, again with Anne MacDougall and Paul Ballou in that same city. It has always been great catching up with Anne over the years.

After I finished my duties with the U.S. Coast Guard, I ran into Jeanne Rheaume on Crane's Beach closer to home. It has always been fun to learn what was happening with each of my past friends since we left Wilmington.

I always ask myself, "Were these connections coincidences?" It was well before the Internet and social media influences. But in every case, our unexpected and unplanned occasions of bumping into one another were a welcoming surprise for both. (I hope!)

And now, through our common community, many of us old friends have re-connected. It's been great feeling that old hometown connection and caring over all those decades and thousands of miles from those days gone by.

Thanks to you all for being an important part of my life. Whether we agree or not, each of you has brought forth only the best memories.

"Come up and see me sometime."
Shared by Alison (Francis) Phaneuf

This picture is the back of a postcard. It was a love note to my grandmother living in East Boston written by my grandfather from his Wilmington camp house at 10 Carter Lane before they were married.

They both had grown up in East Boston, and my grandfather's family had the summer cottage house. He and his Dad, along with his brothers, built a house next door at 12 Carter Lane in 1928. They spent their summers at Silver Lake. My grandparents married in 1939, then moved full time into the 12 Carter Lane.

Both my grandparents were Wilmington icons. My grandmother, Maria Evelyn Govoni Francis, was a sweet soul and worked as a lunch lady at the Boutwell School and the West Intermediate School. She was loved and respected by all the students and staff.

My grandfather, Joe Francis, was a big voice in our community. He was also a Navy Seabee and worked on many building projects for St. Dorothy's Church. I have so many great memories.

The Best Neighborhood

By Becky (Thomas) Lightizer

I grew up at 13 Fairmeadow Road. Maybe a lot of people think they had the best neighborhood, but I know I did!

There had to be about a hundred kids close to my age and there was always something to do. We would fish in the Shawsheen River down the street. Or visit Mrs. White and her goats and guinea hens. Or we'd go blueberry picking up off Nichols Street. Maybe find kids to play Red Rover or tag, or Hide-and-go-Seek.

'Suzy' Peabody even ran a sewing circle for a group of us on her front lawn. Someone always had a knot, but she had the patience of a saint.

If it was raining, we would all crowd into Gedaminsky's carport for a game of Monopoly or Rummy 500. Sometimes we'd run home to get lunch and bring it back to eat together.

It was always exciting when the 'Bug Spray Man' came around on a summer evening. As our Moms were slamming windows shut, we kids ran blindly through the smoke! In the winter we would sled on the sides of the Nichols Street bridge or skate on the frozen sand pits.

Those were the days when we played outside until our parents called us home for dinner. It was safe. Most of the time our parents didn't even know where we were.

My mother passed away from breast cancer when I was only ten years old. The neighborhood was amazing while she was sick, and after she was gone.

Mr. Peters from across the street and my Dad commuted to Cambridge together for thirty-something years. Mrs. Peters was my go-to person if I was home sick or the time when I got a fish hook in my finger.

The whole neighborhood was like an extended family. I spent many afternoons with them, slept over at many of their homes, took trips to the beach and went to the movies with them. Every one of them always made me feel welcome. My Dad and I were incredibly grateful for their kindness.

When I was a little older I was always at the Ingersolls' house. There was always something fun going on there. We'd ride our bikes all the way to the Billerica Mall or Burger Chef in Tewksbury.

One day, my best friend Robin and I were bored so we rode to the Tew-Mac Airport and spent just over twenty dollars to go for a plane ride! We must have been about fifteen at the time.

Dad and I lived in that house until 1987 when he retired and built a home up north and I got married.

I will cherish the wonderful memories and kindness of those neighbors. Always!

"Thank You Wilmington"

Shared by Hank Devlin

I and my brothers and sisters were wards of the State of Massachusetts for most of our lives.

In 1952 I came to live on Dorchester Street, not far from the Shawsheen Elementary School. I was pulled out of that house for a couple of years due to health problems with my foster parents, the Gillis's. Then I remained on Dorchester Street for the rest of my school years.

Without getting into specifics, my home life was not the greatest. But, outside the home growing up in Wilmington was wonderful. I had woods everywhere to explore, the nearby Shawsheen River to swim in, the frozen cranberry bogs to skate on. There were open lots to play baseball and we rode our bikes with baseball cards in the spokes.

I so looked forward going to school and making new friends. I started school in a one room school house. Then I experienced the round school building. Finally, I ended up in my favorite school, Wilmington High.

During my high school years I was lucky to have a great summer job as a lifeguard at Silver Lake. I enjoyed participating in several high school sports and I was fortunate enough to get to know some of the local businesses through the Rotary Club.

I could not have grown up in a better place. Wilmington gave me so much, and for that I will always be grateful.

The Great Escape

As told by Pam Blais

I want to share a story about my youngest sister, Maryann, who is now deceased. When we misbehaved our mother would ground us and we were not allowed to leave our rooms as punishment.

Maryann, though restricted to the house, was determined not to be. So, she tied her bed sheets together, along with the sheets from our other sister's bed in the same room. She then tied one end of the 'rope' to her bed's footboard. Then, holding onto the twisted linen, she jumped out the window.

The bed slid across the room slamming into the wall just below the window. Her aim wasn't the best and my sister landed in one of the trash barrels against the house. She was solidly stuck in the barrel, unable to get herself out.

Our mother had been standing at the kitchen sink washing dishes when suddenly 'something' dropped pass the window. That was so funny!

Remember when...

...it was a real treat to go out to a restaurant

Honorary Mayor of Wilmington
Shared by Fran McLean Donovan

George Spanos was an institution in Wilmington. His nickname was the 'Honorary Mayor of Wilmington.' Of course, that was a given title because we had a Town Manager form of government.

George met his wife in Boston when he first emigrated from Greece. She was Irish and had family in New Hampshire where they married and bought a home. He was a chef at a Boston hotel.

The couple never had children. His love of children was legendary, and every kid who came within ten feet of George got a huge bear hug and a sloppy kiss on the cheek.

George had a big white mustache and a deeply accented voice. You could hear him laugh from across a crowded room!

He helped Bucky and Hazel Bachman develop and staff the Wilmington Skating Club out near the Baldwin Memorial tree on Burlington Avenue. There, in the winter months he spent every weekend helping children lace up their skates.

George opened his diner in Wilmington center in 1937. He strongly supported veterans and active military members in uniform always ate for free at his establishment. The inner walls of his diner were covered with photos of young men in uniform. When they returned home they stopped at George's place for a huge hug and a hot meal.

George closed his diner on Main Street in the late 1950s. Then he came to live with us for a few years in a small studio apartment in our home at Salem Street.

George loved my little brother Frank, and they would often fall asleep while watching TV in his second floor apartment. One night my Mom came screaming down the stairs because George had allowed little six year old Frank to cut an apple with a huge knife, and Frank had deeply cut his hand.

Mom quickly drove my brother to the ER for stitches. George felt horribly guilty. He would often fall asleep smoking cigarettes, and mother was afraid he'd set the house on fire. It seemed after that incident my mother was more watchful of Frank. So, after that George moved into Deming Way, the first elderly housing project in town.

George Spanos well deserved his title of Honorary Mayor of Wilmington.

Bullied
Kathleen O'Brien Weber

Some things happen to you as you grow up and they are often difficult to share. But, here goes.

In the '50s and '60s I lived in Wilmington until I graduated high school in 1971, then I went to college. Our house was diagonally across the street from this boy. He was a terrible bully. He made my family's life miserable as he targeted my sister Donna and my self.

We lived across from the gravel pits, where later the North Intermediate School was built. I have nightmares about that awful boy even to this day.

Some time ago I heard that he had died. I didn't shed a tear. He was an evil boy and sometimes evil gets what it deserves.

I am friends with his sisters, but I don't think they know how he so terrified my sister and I. I do know that his parents knew what he did, but they had no control over his wicked soul. These memories are an unfortunate part of me growing up in what otherwise is a good town.

Years later, most likely due to the traumatizing I went through as a child, I became a therapist specializing in bullying. Bullying must be stopped.

"When Neighbors Were Like Family"

Shared by Karen Lautz Farrell

It was 1955 when my family, the Lautz family, moved into our little ranch house on Kelley Road. It was a dirt road with a dead end off Chandler and Adam Streets. It was only a hop, skip and a jump from the Buzzell, Swain, and Center Schools, and of course, good old Wilmington High School.

My family consisted of my Mom and Dad, my sister Donna and myself. We had no relatives nearby as my Dad was from Connecticut and Mom was an only child from Worcester.

But, in Wilmington it was easy to make friends on our street where the Moms were all stay-at-home housewives and the Dads went off to work each day. We kids spent all our free time running from yard to yard. No one was a stranger back then, and the whole neighborhood was our playground.

Things were going along pretty well for my family. We became friends with the Barrys, the Mutters, the Gingras family, the Cooks, and the O'Reillys from around the corner.

My Mom later gave birth to my youngest sister Leanne and my brother Bob. We became a family of six. My younger siblings, too, ventured out into the neighborhood and became good friends with the Ritchies, the Thackereys, the Drugans, and the Cavanuaghs.

Then, in 1961, our world changed forever! My Dad needed heart valve replacement surgery. After waiting for an available surgeon, he died suddenly in the hospital before his surgery. He was only thirty-eight.

My Mom had to search for a job. She worked in a bakery, sold china, and watched other people's children. She finally landed a decent job at our church as the first secretary for St. Thomas.

Through it all we still had our friends on Kelley Road and Chandler. There was always someone lending a hand, making a meal, offering help when needed.

And there were the Brieres, the Georges, the Lords, the Lanzillos, the Arzilli family, the Poiriers, the Stewarts, and the Henneseys. I'm sure I left out some and am sorry about that.

It was a community that doesn't seem to exist today.

Time went by. There were weddings and funerals. Graduations and new babies. Through it all there was laughter and tears and love. Lots of love.

There were wonderful neighbors who weren't even in our small neighborhood, like the Landrys and the Harveys and the Hanlons.

Whatever happened to towns like this where there were people who cared how their neighbors were doing? Where people weren't afraid to pick up the phone and offer help?

With all our technology we've forgotten how to be 'neighborly.' I am so glad I grew up in Wilmington when I knew my neighbors!

I'm happy to say that even though my siblings and I live out of state now, we can still count many of our old neighborhood friends as our forever friends!

Shenanigans

By Donald Hudson

Wilmington was a great place to grow up. We had places to go fishing, ice skating, swimming, and many other outdoors activities. There were plenty of other kids to play games and shenanigans with too, but it wasn't a city.

We did get into many shenanigans, usually harmless pranks or high jinks. We would climb up a large cedar tree on West Street where we could hide out of site. Sometimes we would throw rotten tomatoes at passing cars until one hit a police car. (Not a very good idea.) We hid there for a long time while the police looked in the brush and woods for whoever tossed the tomatoes.

One night we poured a bit of gasoline into a Jack-o-lantern and lit it up as cars came around the corner. Some drivers cursed at us and some laughed. But when it was my turn, red and blue flashing lights came on when I dropped the match into the Jack-o-lantern and flames shot out of its eyes and mouth.

We all ran through the nearby swamp, but the police officers chasing us didn't know the swamp like we kids did. Later, we saw the same police at

Elia's store. They were covered in mud and muck. We were relatively clean since we knew where not to step as we escaped.

We also stripped the elastic bands from a golf ball and stretched it across West Street at night. That was fun until someone got the bright idea of hanging a sheet of newspaper over the elastic band. Not so good, as the first car that came around the corner slid to a sideways stop out of fear. We apologized to the driver and promptly removed the elastic bands and newspaper while the driver laughed at us.

There was an older lady in our neighborhood who owned a Renault Dauphine, a car smaller than a VW bug. We would regularly pick it up and turn it sideways in her driveway. One night she saw us at Elia's and politely asked us to please lift the front end when rotating her car so as not to get the front wheels locked. Otherwise, apparently she didn't mind our nightly prank. Well, we never again bothered her car, and watched out for her and her property.

There was this one guy, though, who was always complaining about us kids playing basketball in the street. He had a small car as well, a Karmann Ghia. It got moved to his front stoop along with a flaming bag of doggie poo. One of us rang his door bell and ran like crazy. He was not a happy camper and called the police while we hid in the woods across the street.

By the way, we continued to play basketball in the road.

We did a lot more good things, though, like shoveling snow and cutting lawns for the elderly in the neighborhood.

A Salute to John Rich
Fallen Heroes: Part IV
By Fred Shine

Young John Allen Rich was a typical, fun-loving Wilmington kid of the 1960s. He hung out with his friends Bobby Carney and Larry Pinto. He enjoyed running fast cars.

A funny thing happened at WHS in the boy's bathroom located at the top ramp to the Adams Street wing. John, Bobby, and Larry, and a couple other guys went into the bathroom.

Obviously, growing up we all knew the boy's room was where you would go to 'sneak a smoke'. It was there, I heard, that Bobby lit a cherry bomb and tossed it to John. John caught the powerful firecracker, and in a panic, hoping to put it out, threw it in a toilet.

It didn't go out and exploded, blowing the toilet to pieces and sending water out the door and down the stairway. All the boys were caught and got in trouble. They each got detention, had to clean up the soaking mess, and replace the toilet. If they did that today they would be sent to jail.

Right after graduating, John had married his high school sweetheart. His wife was not in favor of the Vietnam War and didn't want her new husband to enter the military. That was one of the reasons she persuaded him to marry her. Well, the marriage didn't really work out, and soon after the wedding they separated and his wife filed for divorce.

John ended up in the USMC and soon shipped out to Nam. He was still only separated, the divorce not finalized yet, which left his wife as his 'legal next of kin' when he was killed over there.

John's parents had moved to Mesa, Arizona. After their son had been killed, the Marines contacted the soldier's documented next of kin, and John's estranged wife had been presented with her husband's military medals and a monetary benefit.

The wife apparently refused to accept responsibility for his body and refused to take part in anything to do with his burial. John's body was then claimed by his parents and was buried in Mesa, Arizona.

When John's dad passed away, I believe in the late 1970s, John's remains were exhumed and returned to Wilmington to be buried beside his father in the family grave. John's body is not in the "Field of Crosses," which is why there was no bronze marker located there. For over 53 years John's resting site was very often overlooked on Memorial Day when flags and flowers were placed on the graves.

I tried for many, many years to get his bronze marker. I got some assistance from the Wilmington Veterans officer, but it never seemed to go anywhere. Now, I have been trying for over 30 years to get John's bronze marker, and it was the last promise I made to myself to get it done.

So, feeling that John would not get his official military bronze marker, this past May I took money I had saved up and purchased John's marker myself. I had it placed in the Field of Crosses. It was something the town of Wilmington should have done 53 years ago.

Then in August, the government did approve John's full military bronze marker and I had it placed over John's remains, in his family lot. A few years ago, with the help of Danny Sullivan, another "Lake Kid" who worked for AVCO as well, we had all John's medals reissued and framed. We presented them to the family at the re-dedication of John's Memorial.

The Egg Route

Shared by Denise (Lynch) Robarge

I grew up on Cottage Street in Wilmington where my dad, Willie Lynch, a thirty year police officer in town, built our home. Dad also grew up on the same street.

On Saturday mornings my grand-dad, Art Lynch, would pick up my sisters and I, and we would go on "The Egg Route." We would drive our Nana, Fran Lynch, to the Lion's Den hair salon to get her weekly hair permanent. Then we would go to the Wildwood Street farm and pick up several dozen eggs to be delivered to my grand-dad's siblings.

We would go over to my Great-Uncle Paul Lynch's house first. He was the Wilmington Chief of Police. Then we'd go to my Great-Uncle William "Snaper" Lynch's place. I remembered he worked on the B & M Railroad.

The last house was always Great-Uncle Alfred Lynch's on Middlesex Ave where we would play in the barn with the wild kittens. Uncle Alfred was married to Eleanor Cavanaugh. Remember Cavanaugh's Funeral Home? My sisters and I thought she was a movie star because she smoked cigarettes with a filter.

After grand-dad had his two fingers of whiskey with Uncle Alfred, he would take us to

Ricky's Dog House. Sometime later, after Ricky's closed down, we would go to Jack-In-The-Box.

When we were done eating, we'd go back to the Lion's Den to pick up Nana. If she wasn't ready, we'd listen to Irish music with grand-dad in the car.

The Egg Route on Saturday was the best day of the week.

Remember when...

...we cooked popcorn in a wire basket

Mrs. T

Shared by her son, Ryan Tildsley

I would like to honor my own mother. Members of my family are lifelong residents of Wilmington. My mother impacted our town in a variety of ways. She was known as Mrs. T, the nicest lady in Wilmington.

My mother Carol is 63 years old, and unfortunately, recently suffered a major stroke and is in critical condition. We are not sure if she's going to pull through, but I am inclined now to honor her in this book.

She worked at the North Wilmington Dunkin' Donuts for thirteen years and always made everyone smile, maybe with an extra free donut or two in your bag. She also worked at all the Wilmington schools as a lunch lady. Lastly, she worked for almost ten years as an after-school teacher for the town's CARES program.

Everyone loved her, and she made such a big impact on many students and co-workers, but especially me.

Photo of Carol Tildsley and her grandson Logan
*Unfortunately, Carol succumbed to her illness this February. May she rest in peace.

Making a Difference

By Those Who Cared

Now, at the end of our group book, is an appropriate time to mention the many notable people who lived in or are from Wilmington who impacted our small neighborhoods and its residents.

Over the years we as a community have been affected by these noteworthy people, including our parents and family members, our friends and neighbors, our teachers and other students, the local business owners and town leaders.

In honor of these great human beings who taught us and inspired us and mentored us and helped us along the way, we all would like to give tribute to those who influenced us and made ***Wilmington, Our Town.***

George Keith

There are three teachers I think need to be mentioned here. My third grade teacher, Mrs. Malarkey; my fourth grade teacher, Mrs. Jennings; and my sixth grade teacher Mr. Tildsley. They were the kind of teachers who made a difference in my life and made school fun to go to.

Trish Jennings
I still laugh when I think about how Mr. Tildsley would bat for me and hit the ball out of the park when we played softball. I was such a slow runner the opposing team could actually get the ball back and get me out before I got to home base. It was hysterical.

Kathleen Gilligan
I would like to nominate my dad, Joe Gilligan. He was a teacher and coach, and influenced so many with his wry, dry humorous way of persuading students and athletes to strive for their best. He was a gifted teacher and loved his vocation.

Doug Dayton
Mr. Gilligan was a role model for us students.

Deborah Hall Shanteler
Mr. Gilligan was one of those teachers who everyone remembers as one of the best. I loved his classes and felt lucky to have him as a teacher.

Alison (Francis) Phaneuf
Mr. Wilbur Sparks. I fondly remember Mr. Sparks riding his three-wheel bicycle, rain or shine, to and from his different janitor jobs. He was always smiling and saying "Hi" and waving

to everyone. You couldn't help but smile when you saw him peddling so happily around our wonderful town. He spoke so nicely of his wife. He was one of the great, for sure!

Laurie Carrasco Lowman
I would love to have my Dad mentioned here. Frustuoso (Rudy, as he was known in town) Carrasco. He was in every veteran organization and had Memorial Day dedicated to him the year after he died.

Janet Witham Hawes
I would suggest Mr. Breakey, a wonderful guidance counselor, as well as Mr. Gilligan who really lit up biology for me. Also, Mr. Eager, my Latin teacher. My large vocabulary is due to my three years of Latin with him.

Linda Aspeslagh
Mr. Breakey also taught me to drive and was oh so patient.

Mark Bartnick
I remember when I was in the fifth grade at Swain School and Mr. Tildsley was teaching his class down the end of the hall. Well, I used to go by his room when he was teaching on my way to the bathroom. Every time I'd peek into his class door window. One day I guess he got sick of me coming by and peeking in, so he came out to the

hall and pulled me into his class. Then he asked me if I had leaky pipes! Of course, I said "No." Well, he said something like, "You keep going to the bathroom like five times a day." The whole class started cracking up. Boy, was I embarrassed!

Sue Landers McNamara
I have to add Mrs. Russo our neighbor who on Sept. 26, 1969 came to the Landers' house on Clark Street and tried to give CPR to members of my family who had been removed from the burning house. So thankful for her attempts!

Cathy Fantasia Seely
The dramatic social studies teacher, 'Daddy' Roche. His frequent phrases were "all set good people" and "your heads will roll."

Ellen Balser Kimble
My Dad, Foster Balser, was honored for his forty-five years of service to the Boys Scouts of America and his assisting the groups of Girl Scouts and the Campfire Girls. He was a long time Scoutmaster of Wilmington's Troop 56. He was also instrumental in acquiring land near the Andover town line to set up the Wilmington Youth Camp.

Kathleen Bell
Mrs. Webber, head of the high school business department for many years. She was active in town politics and helped many students on a personal level, but never let it been known.

Karin Passmore
I'd like to mention Adele Passmore who was very instrumental in developing the Historical Commission's work at Harnden Tavern and who also wrote a book on the history of Wilmington.

Bob Johnson
I'd like to mention an old friend of mine, Fred Shine, who has devoted much of his life to supporting local veterans and honoring fallen heroes of Wilmington.

Valerie Clark
I would like to nominate my mother, Nancy H. Clark. She served on the school committee and wrote a column called 'Nosey Nancy' for the Town Crier for many years, bringing news from all over the town to share. For years she also sold real estate out of the train station in the center of Wilmington. She was a great supporter of the town's veterans. She also helped whoever she could, whenever she could. Her motto was: 'Plant a seed of goodness in someone and one day they will bloom and plant a seed in someone else.'

Terrijoan (Marden) Bello
My father, Tom Marden, moved to Wilmington around 1960, but has recently passed. He was very involved in the Veteran's Memorial services at the town Common and the 4th of July festivities.

Ed Palino
I played high school football for Joe Gilligan from 1956 through 1960. He was a great teacher, coach, mentor and friend.

Elizabeth Briana
Michele (Caira) Nortonen was my favorite teacher. I was fascinated that she had worked with the Navajos and I was lucky to have her in the third and sixth grades at Woburn Street School. I remember loving school in the third grade because she provided something I needed when my family was falling apart. She later became a principal, then I lost track of her since I no longer live in Wilmington. I went on to become a teacher (and now principal). She had a huge impact on me.

Elizabeth Gilligan Cavanaugh
My dad, James (Jimmy) Gilligan, a Boston school teacher, took the train into the city every day. For many years he was a member of the Lake Betterment Association in the building on

the other side of Main Street across from Silver Lake.

He started the Wilmington Athletic Development Association (WADA) for young men to play baseball in the park south of town next to the railroad. He also introduced sports into the High School, starting with baseball. He spent several years as a town selectman, including a stint as chairman. All of his adult life he was involved in local politics and the youth.

Shirley Pumfrey
I had Dr. Fagan as my physician. He used to come to my house when I could not get to him. I always thought I would be dead before he walked into the house. Of course, he was older at the time.

Tanya Coy Shiner
How about 'Mac' from McNamara Tire in Wilmington? He did a lot to support our town. He gave many young men work by hiring them at his shop. I remember when he bought matching shirts for my brother's Little League team. Apparently they didn't have uniforms in those days.

George Keith
Coach Fred Bellissimo was a great guy. He would let me skip study and go to the gym. I wish I got to play football for him.

Lisa DiCecca

Ms. Linda Marinel was my second grade teacher at the Whitefield School in the 1973-74 school year. She was an incredible teacher. She gave out marbles as prizes and we played with them in the school yard. She taught us to square dance, read 'Charlotte's Web' to us out under the big tree out front, and taught us the song 'Shoo Fly, Don't Bother Me.' I could go on and on. She was the best!

Rose Chase

I have a memory about taking Driver's Ed with Mr. Demos. I remember him taking us on Highway 93 before it was opened and learning how to maneuver the ramps. I was so good at it that he promised to enter me in the Indy 500. He often said he wished he had a hard hat during our driving lessons. The look on his face when I got my license was priceless! He was a great teacher. It took a lot of guts to teach us to drive.

Ann Berghaus
How about Gerald 'Scratch' O'Reilly, the high school star on the field? He grew up at the lake. Heading up to Lowell his house is still there on the left, half of it on the Wilmington side and the other half on the Tewksbury side. He also authored many books on Wilmington.

Valerie Clark
I would also like to nominate Larz Neilson who ran and edited the newspaper. He is a great historian of Wilmington and continues to this day to keep us amazed with history of the people and places in town.

Lusann Wishart
Dan Spriggs was an amazing and very dedicated science and biology teacher at the North Intermediate School.

Chris DiCecca
Frank Lentine was a great teacher, coach, mentor and friend to many students and athletes over the years. He had a major impact on many young lives in Wilmington. Those who had the good fortune of having Frank in their lives are very grateful.

Tom Walsh
The Elia's and Lucci's families. Through their stores they still help a lot of struggling families weekly. Still keeping Wilmington with the small town feel.

Kathleen Bell
Mr. Kelley, the legendary math teacher. In my senior year I was in his class when a student from Mr. Sullivan's class came in requesting a slide rule. Well, there was a six foot display model in the closet. Naturally, Mr. Kelley had the little freshman carry it back over his shoulder. When he returned for a smaller one, Mr. Kelley broke out into a huge grin. He happened to be wearing his slide rule tie tack that day. He sent it carried aloft by two of the biggest guys in the class!

Kevin Burke
Jim Stewart for two reasons. First, for expertly keeping the town meetings moving along and on schedule. Second, as quarterback of the 1976 Super Bowl team.

Patricia Toner
Mrs. Rogers, the sixth grade teacher at Woburn Street School. Yup, I remembered what a noun was after she threw that eraser at me!

Paul Burke
Howie LeFavour, who started the WRBL (Wilmington Rec Basketball League) and Bob Dicey who continued the efforts from the '60s into the '80s.

Doreen Scolastico Riley
Miss Kalill, the music teacher at the North. She was very cool and classy. I always remember she wore great smelling perfume too.

Lillian Halpin Robinson
Mr. Sullivan was one of my favorite teachers. He taught us how to make Baked Alaska and let me knit in class.

Jeff Irwin
Kathleen Bell was a kind and responsive HS teacher. I always had to put in so much extra time to understand math. She was willing to help get that job done. I'm sure her influence helped steer me into a thirty-seven year teaching career with special needs students. Thank you for being so caring.

Trish Jennings
Ms. Bell. You were a great teacher! I remember how respectful you were and talked to us like we were mature people. Loved your class. Thanks!

Mike Barcellos
My father-in-law, Lester White, member of the School Committee, Wilmington Nice Guy Award winner, and all around a good guy, used to say to my kids when they complained: *"Oh, stop complaining. When I was a kid in Vermont, I used to walk three miles to school and back, up hill both ways!"*

Lisa Stira
Kathleen Bell made sure we all understood, and never humiliated or patronized those who were struggling.

Vincent Ruggiero
Forest Dame, a great mechanic. I bought my first car in 1974. It was a '64 Corvette coupe. Forest was the only one, other than my self, I let work on it. I still own that car thanks to Forest teaching me many things.

Doug Dayton
Ok, I offer William P Dayton for his lifetime as a Wilmington resident. He was my father who went to most of the town meetings, provided valuable insight to Apples Society, and did an enormous amount time researching the Dayton family tree. He was born in Wilmington at the Snug Harbor house on Burlington Ave, not far from where he lived for most of my childhood.

At that time Wilmington was a small town community, so everyone knew everyone. We did not own a car, so my dad walked to the train station every day, snow, rain, sunny, hot and cold, for 45 plus years while working at Stone and Webster Engineering Co. He was a mentor to me when I started there in 1967. Wilmington meant a lot to him, and his input into events were well received by his friends, colleges and family.

He loved the town and people he grew up with while in town. He left me with lots of good memories of Wilmington and the people. He also left me a lot of historical information about the town. I've been permanently gone from Wilmington since 1985, but have great memories of our time there. Wilmington was a great place to grow up in.

AnnMarie Mahoney
I'd like to say a few words about Dr. Fagan. I was three or four when Dr. Fagan made house calls at the Mahoney family household on Fairfield Road. I remember him as a big man all dressed in black, including his medical bag. I was the youngest of eight, so you can imagine a bunch of kids running around him. I'd follow behind him when he walked through the house waddling like a duck. I assume now it was due to his age. Those were fond memories of happier times.

Tom Beaton

I like to mention my dad, Joe Beaton, who taught for many years at Wilmington High School. He loved kids, and teaching was the perfect job for him.

John Dineen

You might be from Wilmington if you had your hair cut by Rick Allen. After forty-three years of keeping the men and boys of Wilmington looking sharp, Rick recently decided to retire and shut down his Middlesex Ave barber shop. Rick, who is moving out of state, is a life-long town resident. He followed his father's (Ralph) footsteps, who was also a town barber for forty-five years.

Lois (Hinxman) Grant

I would like to nominate my father, Walter (Diz) Hinxman and my Uncle Bucky Backman for starting the Wilmington Skating Club behind the South School on Chestnut Street.

George Spanos, Mike Weinberg, Tom Galvin, my dad and uncle, and I believe Art Spears, were the original members of the board of directors. There might have been more, but I don't remember and don't want to slight anyone!

They had many meetings in the South School. They also had spaghetti dinners and baked bean suppers as fundraisers to help with the club's expenses. The gatherings were always well attended and enjoyed. The club also held strawberry shortcake festivals and Halloween parties. They are so many happy memories.

We lived right across the street. One day Dad and Uncle Bucky rented a bulldozer and knocked down some trees, dug out the rink, and built the fence.

I'm sure not many people know that my mom almost got killed while taking them lunch one day. Bucky Junior was working a tree when it snapped and flew over her, throwing her into the mud. The heavy tree rode up her back toward her neck. Thankfully it missed her head. It was a strange accident and she was very bruised and sore, but also very lucky. Family and close neighbors treated her like a queen for a good two weeks after the accident.

I'm not trying to take anything away from the club officers, but in the end they pretty much built the rink by themselves, and I watched it. We had years of fun playing ice hockey and skating there. Many kids went to that rink to enjoy the effort of so many good men. I am sorry to boast so much, but I'm very proud of them. There are so many happy memories of that rink.

Donald C. Hubbard

I remember the incredible Larry Cushing. He looked for me in school to personally apologize for the boxing decision that went against me in my match with Danny Rheaume the previous night. He told me I had won that fight easily and couldn't understand how they voted the way they did. Loved that guy.

Peter Orlando

Ms. Fields, my favorite teacher in the third grade at Buzzell School, then Mrs. Jennings in the fourth at the Swain.

Marc Bliss

I've been reluctant to mention my parents because they would probably bristle at this. Aside from my mother playing piano concerts, they avoided the limelight. However, growing up in their house I witnessed their efforts for the betterment of Wilmington.

About seventy years ago my mother joined with Larry Cushing and others to establish the Wilmington Recreation Commission. My father served on building committees of the now razed high school, the Adams Street extension to the high school, and the current library (the tree planted in the front of the library is in his honor). He also served a term as a town selectman.

My dad was the Congregational Church moderator and joined with town clergy to encourage an ecumenical movement among the town's houses of worship. He also started the chapter of Kiwanis and rose to Lt. Governor.

Growing up in their house and in the town of Wilmington makes me happy and proud.

Barbara Bianchi
My grandmother Helen Allen, who spent many years helping junior high kids with their reading. I remember going with her to help with Micelli's campaign. She was born in 1900 and drove until she was 95.

Ann Berghaus
Wilmington has been blessed with soooo many wonderful characters who have contributed to the greatness of our Town. It's a difficult task to list them all.

Remember when...

...the entire family ate dinner together

Final Thoughts

Well, we did it! Our book is finally completed. The support and encouragement from so many people has been absolutely amazing. It's been a terrific group effort. We've read stories from dozens of Wilmington residents, past and present. We've also viewed memories and comments from hundreds of others who were there beside us.

Throughout these pages we've re-lived our past experiences growing up in a wonderful town. We've revisited the things which were important to us. We've pondered the good things in our youth and remembered some of the not so good events as well.

This book is a mirror of our younger lives. It reveals who we were and defines who we are now. It explains the simple terms of life in a unique place. It reflects the goodness of friends and neighbors and teachers and parents who molded us into decent, principled citizens.

If I had initially known how much time it would have taken to put this collection together, I may have decided against it. But probably not. There were times, though, when I felt like one of our mean old English teachers telling his students to get their homework in on time. But every one of you came through.

In fact, it has been a pleasure working with each of you. Reading your memorable stories has certainly transformed me back to the good ole days. Listening to your heartfelt accounts from the past has touched me. Editing your funny tales of mischief and tomfoolery brought a welcomed smile to my face. And looking through your private written thoughts has humbled me and made me realize how fragile life is.

I respect every one of you for being part of an exceptional experience and for being who you have become. New England-strong comes to mind. I'll say it one more time. I am proud to be in your company.

Finally, I want to explain something to all of you. I've been asked several times, "Why?" Why did I begin this project? Why did I pursue such a risky and time-consuming task?

Let me tell you why.

Several years ago I was teaching Career-Infused English Language Acquisition (a unique form of ESL) classes at the local Cochise Community College here in southern Arizona. I had a very diverse group of twelve adult students in my intermediate level class.

They came from nine different countries and spoke five different native languages. An engineer from Puerto Rico, a young determined worker from Vietnam, an artist from Guatemala, an office manager from Ecuador, a young man from the rice fields of Cambodia, a military officer from Korea, a veterinarian from Peru, a security supervisor from Afghanistan, business owners from Mexico, and young women from south of the border doing their best.

They were intelligent, ambitious learners wanting to better their lives and the lives of their families. They were uncomplaining risk takers willing to take the journey of their lives as they immigrated to America.

So, one day our department director told all the instructors that she wanted us to complete a class project prior to the Christmas break, only six weeks away. I'd been teaching there long enough to have seen other 'class projects.' A class song, a simple skit, a short video or montage of photos from a field trip.

All 'fluff.' Things that really don't mean much. Things that don't make an impact. Things that aren't long-lasting. I'm not into 'fluff.' I'm into results. I'm into doing things that can make a life-long impression. I'm into things that make a difference.

I told my students about the assignment. I wanted them to write a short story about their lives and their journeys to the United States. Nothing elaborate, just a few pages. Of course they weren't too thrilled about the long homework. "Oh teacher, too much work!" they said. So I sweetened the deal and asked, "What if all of you write your story, then we put them together and have them published in a book?"

Instantly every person was on board. It was an experiment in goal setting, the foundation of our classes. Task, hard work, deadline, all of which we focused on in school.

The problem was that to write, edit (numerous times), proof read, format, print, and deliver such a book in less than six weeks seemed an impossible task. But this project was important to my students. And to me. This was the first time in their lives they had been asked to share their stories and most likely the only time they would be in print.

You see, I knew what they had all gone through. I knew about their struggles and their fears. I knew about their dreams for the future. But I wanted them to tell us.

Every day they worked on their stories. Every day we made corrections and revisions. Every day my students wanted to add more to their stories. Every day we grew closer to finishing their book, a project which I don't think has ever been done before.

Two days before the deadline, boxes of my students' books arrived. Without a doubt it was one of the most impressive achievements in their lives. They were excited and proud, as they should have been, for what they had completed.

They were confident student-authors with their new book, ***Our Stories* by The Dream Makers.**

Everyone has a voice to be heard. And everyone has a story to tell. And that, my friends, is why I wanted you to write this book.

Thank you, Bob Johnson

Made in the USA
Middletown, DE
18 April 2021